The

HERITAGE
BOOK

1 9 9 8

The
HERITAGE
BOOK
1 9 9 8

Edna McCann

Prentice Hall Canada Inc.
Scarborough, Ontario

Prentice-Hall, Inc., Upper Saddle River, New Jersey
Prentice-Hall International (UK) Limited, London
Prentice-Hall of Australia, Pty. Limited, Sydney
Prentice-Hall Hispanoamericana, S.A., Mexico City
Prentice-Hall of India Private Limited, New Delhi
Prentice-Hall of Japan, Inc., Tokyo
Simon & Schuster Southeast Asia Private Limited, Singapore
Editora Prentice-Hall do Brasil, Ltda., Rio de Janeiro

ISBN 0-13-891227-0

Acquisitions Editor: Jill Lambert
Managing Editor: Robert Harris
Copy Editor: Kate Forster, Kelli Howey
Production Editor: Mary Ann McCutcheon
Production Coordinator: Julie Preston
Art Direction: Mary Opper
Cover Design: Julia Hall
Cover Image: Gord Handley
Page Layout: April Haisell

1 2 3 4 5   02 01 00 99 98

Printed and bound in Canada

Literary Credits

Page 2 "Let the Winds of Winter Bluster!" by Charles S. Kinnison from
Wintertime Ideals, Vol. 20, No. 1 (Milwaukee, Wisconsin: Ideals
Publishing, 1963), page 2.

Page 15 "Dust of Snow" by Robert Frost from *The Poetry of Robert
Frost* (New York: Henry Holt and Company, Inc., 1969).

Page 29 "An Evening Prayer" by Avery Brooke from *Plain Prayers in a
Complicated World* (Boston: Cowley, 1993).

Page 37 "March" by Hume Wilkins from *Every Day Is a Gift*. (Ayr,
Ontario: Ayr News).

Page 68 "The Courage That My Mother Had" by Edna St. Vincent
Millay. From *Collected Poems*, HarperCollins. Copyright © 1954, 1982
by Norma Millay Ellis. All rights reserved. Reprinted by permission of
Elizabeth Barnett, literary executor.

Page 97 "Many Things to Me" by Jay Giammarino from *Ideals Country*,
Vol. 48, No. 4 (Menasha, Wisconsin: Banta Co., 1991).

THE HERITAGE BOOK

Photo Credits

Winter	Spring
Florence Gillespie	Florence Gillespie
Charlene Daley	Charlene Daley
Florence Gillespie	Gord Handley
Gord Handley	Florence Gillespie
Charlene Daley	Florence Gillespie
Gord Handley	Gord Handley
Charlene Daley	Gord Handley
Gord Handley	Gord Handley

Summer	Autumn
Charlene Daley	Gord Handley
Vince Farr	Charlene Daley
Gord Handley	Vince Farr
Vince Farr	Charlene Daley
Charlene Daley	Gord Handley
Florence Gillespie	Florence Gillespie
Charlene Daley	Charlene Daley
Charlene Daley	Charlene Daley

Introduction

While writing the 1998 edition of *The Heritage Book* I have been reminded time after time that every day is truly a gift. Whether it be in the form of love shared, a joy discovered, a comfort bestowed or a lesson learned, each day brings some experience that enriches our lives. Some gifts we may take for granted, and others strike us poignantly. Some gifts come in brightly wrapped packages that bring smiles to our faces. Others are gifts of spirit, which are special and enduring enough to reinforce the belief that the world is a truly wonderful place.

Thank you to all of my readers who have given me so much over the years — may this book be my gift to you. I wish you all a year touched with many blessings.

Edna McCann

January

Thursday January 1

The Roman god Janus, from whom we have derived the word January, was known as the "deity of good beginnings." What better way to start the year than with a "good beginning."

The temple of Janus in Rome featured a two-faced statue of the god with the young visage looking east and the old one looking west.

On this first day of the new year we could be as the statue of Janus, looking back to appreciate our accomplishments and our many blessings and then looking ahead to make plans and set our goals for the year to come.

With faith and enthusiasm many things are possible. May I wish to each and every one of you a most happy and successful new year.

Friday January 2

Don't judge those who try and fail. Judge only those who fail to try.

Saturday January 3

Let the winds of winter bluster!
Let 'em howl and let 'em whine!
Let 'em all their forces muster
In a wild and twisting line!
Let 'em, with my comfort, wrestle,
Let the snowflakes fill the air!
By the fireside I will nestle
In my big old easy chair!

In a book my nose I'll bury
As the wind around me roars,
While the wings of fancy carry me
To sun-lit balmy shores!
I will be a lazy rover,
I will sail the balmy seas,
I will roam the country over,
In my fancy, at my ease!

Let the blizzards bang the shutters
Till complainingly they squeak,
Let 'em twist around the gutters
With a wild and whining shriek—
I declare I'll hardly hear it!
I'll be roaming far away
In adventure-seeking spirit,
While I let my fancy play!

Charles S. Kinnison's words described my day
perfectly—a fire, a comfy chair and a good book.

Sunday January 4

And God blessed the seventh day, and sanctified it: because that in it he had rested from all his work which God created and made.

Genesis 2:3

Monday January 5

After the hectic pace of the holiday season it feels good to have some days with few, if any, planned activities.

A large family is a great blessing and I certainly delight in our time together. I also treasure my time alone. Thanks to my advanced years I am able to enjoy both without appearing to be cranky. Whenever the festivities become too much for me I simply say "Well, I think that I need a nap if I'm to enjoy our dinner/party/conversation/walk etc. later, so I'll rejoin you in a little while."

I slip off to my room for a short time and then I am able to return in a rejuvenated frame of mind ready to be a part of whatever may be happening. The nice thing is that people expect the elderly to nap more frequently so one needn't feel like a "wet blanket" when removing oneself from the inevitable chaos that develops at a large "gathering of the clan." Of course this really only works well in your own home. It's quite difficult to sneak away when visiting elsewhere—although I did see my son-in-law Bruce hide out in his car after a particularly long and tiring visit with the grandchildren.

Occasionally we all need a break!

Tuesday January 6

In the Western Church today is the celebration of the Epiphany, the coming of the Magi to celebrate the birth of Christ. In many countries, in the tradition of the Three Kings, the custom of giving gifts will be repeated today as it has been for many centuries.

A merry Christmas to my many European friends who celebrate on this day.

Wednesday January 7

Faith, like light, should always be simple and unbending; while love, like warmth, should beam forth on every side, and bend to every necessity of our brother.

Martin Luther

Thursday January 8

Andy Rooney once said, "The two biggest sellers in any bookstore are the cookbooks and the diet books. The cookbooks tell you how to prepare the food and the diet books tell you how not to eat any of it."

Eating (or not eating) at this time of year is sometimes quite stressful. Many of us have made a new year's resolution to lose weight and become healthier. Magazines have articles that boast "Lose 12 pounds this week on our mini-fast diet" or "Lose 4 pounds by this weekend."

According to health experts, the best way to lose weight is to eat less fat, reduce the size of your food portions, drink 6–8 glasses of water per day and look for a gradual loss of 1–2 pounds per week: "You didn't gain weight overnight, so you can't expect to lose it overnight."

A little trick that I've learned over the years is to use raw vegetables as snacks. Green beans, broccoli, celery, cauliflower, cucumbers, carrots, mushrooms, or bell peppers with 2 tablespoons of "skinny dip" (3/4 cup plain low-fat yogurt, 1 tbsp. each fresh chives and chopped garlic, 1/4 cup minced red onion) help keep you feeling full and satisfied and keep hunger pangs away.

My son-in-law said it best: "But Mother, I *like* to eat!"

Friday January 9

Far better it is to dare mighty things, to win glorious triumphs even though checkered by failure, than to rank with those poor spirits who neither enjoy much nor suffer much, because they live in the gray twilight that knows not victory nor defeat.

Theodore Roosevelt

Saturday January 10

The sunshine on a winter day
Is ever soft and fair,
And in a very tender way
It warms the winter air.
There's laughter in my heart and soul,
I never mind a thing...
I thank God for the winter sun
For then I dream of spring.

Garnett Ann Shultz

Sunday January 11

He that dwelleth in the secret place of the most High shall abide under the shadow of the Almighty. I will say of the Lord, He is my refuge and my fortress: my God; in him will I trust.

Psalms 91:1–2

Monday January 12

Is there anything more frustrating than a product purchased that doesn't meet your expectations? Sometimes it is as simple as a container of milk that is sour before an expiry date. Other times it may be a sweater whose colours have run together or an appliance that won't work. Whatever your problem, there are ways to complain to the seller that will nearly always result in your satisfaction.

1. State your problem in a matter-of-fact manner. Explain what you bought and what went wrong.
2. If possible, type your letter and keep it to one page in length.
3. Try to be complimentary. Explain that you have used their products before (if that is true) and have come to expect fine quality but now you have a problem.
4. Include your address and phone number so that someone can get in touch with you.
5. Be courteous. Outline what you want the company to do.
6. Go to the top. Address your letter to the president of the company.

Tuesday January 13

H ope is wishing for a thing to come true; faith is believing that it will come true.

Norman Vincent Peale

Wednesday January 14

I f you wish success in life, make perseverance your bosom friend, experience your wise counselor, conscience your elder brother, and hope your guardian genius.

Joseph Addison

Thursday January 15

T his is the birthdate of Dr. Martin Luther King Jr., the great African-American statesman. In his speech of December 11, 1964, accepting the Nobel Peace Prize, he said, "Nonviolence is the answer to the crucial political and moral questions of our time; the need for man to overcome oppression and violence without resorting to oppression and violence.

"Man must evolve for all human conflict a method which rejects revenge, aggression and retaliation. The foundation of such a method is love."

Friday January 16

I was a great admirer of Sir Winston Churchill and his wife Lady Churchill. My son-in-law John recounted this interesting bit of information to me. Perhaps you readers old enough to remember the Churchills will find it of interest as well.

Lady Churchill was ninety-two years old when she passed away. When the many years of widowhood had greatly diminished her financial resources, she decided to sell some of her family treasures. When this became known, a member of parliament suggested that Lady Churchill be given a special state pension as a token of the nation's gratitude to this great lady.

She would not consider this and continued with the sale. Independent and dignified to the end, Lady Churchill represented all that was so fine in her generation.

Saturday January 17

When you make new friends, don't forget the old.
One is silver, the other gold.

Erasmus

Sunday January 18

Be strong and of a good courage; be not afraid, neither be thou dismayed: for the Lord thy God is with thee whithersoever thou goest.

Joshua 1:9

Monday January 19

My dear friend Jake Frampton stopped in for dinner this evening. As my former readers know, Jake owns a bookstore and he spoils me frequently by bringing over books from authors old and new for me to enjoy.

One of my favourite types of books to read is the suspense novel, and who writes these spine-tinglers better than Mary Higgins Clark?

Ms. Clark was born and raised in New York City and is a graduate of Fordham University. She now lives in Saddle River, New Jersey.

Author of more than a dozen novels and short story collections, she is a superb story teller who creates nightmarish situations that lie just beneath the surface of ordinary life.

All of her books have been major bestsellers, and once started they are nearly impossible to put down. I look forward to an evening of terror!

Tuesday January 20

I find the great thing in this world is not so much where we stand, as in what direction we are moving: to reach the port of heaven, we must sail sometimes with the wind and sometimes against it—but we must sail, and not drift, nor lie at anchor.

Oliver Wendell Holmes

Wednesday January 21

Middle age is the time when the narrow waist and the broad mind begin to change places.

Thursday January 22

When we must accept a hardship
That we did not dream could be
Our first impulse is to ask,
Why me? O, God why me?
When a blessing comes to us,
We receive it joyously,
When seldom do we question,
Why me? O God, why me?

Nellie Knuth

Friday January 23

On a cold winter's evening is there anything more delicious than a bowl of hot soup? One of my favourites is potato and bacon soup, a tasty treat that can be a meal when served with hot bread, a wedge of cheddar cheese and a salad.

4 tbsp. butter
2 tbsp. vegetable oil
6 medium potatoes, peeled and cut into cubes
4 medium onions, peeled and thinly sliced
6 cups basic stock (or chicken stock) all fat removed
3 tsp. salt
1/2 tsp. pepper
1/2 lb. bacon, cut into 1-inch pieces
1/2 cup grated Parmesan cheese

Heat butter and vegetable oil in a large heavy pot. When hot, add potatoes. Cook over medium heat 10 minutes, turning often. Add onions. Fry until both are golden brown. Add stock, salt and pepper. Cover with a loose-fitting lid and reduce heat. Simmer for 30 minutes or until potatoes are soft.

Meanwhile fry bacon pieces until crisp. Drain on paper towel and crumble into fine bits.

Ladle the hot soup into heated soup bowls and sprinkle each with a heaping tablespoon of bacon and one of Parmesan cheese.
Serves 6–8.

Saturday January 24

In the 1840s Irish and English immigrants established the hamlet of Tyrone, north of Bowmanville. At that time the area around Bowmanville and Oshawa was a growing agricultural community. The water-powered mill was built in 1846 to grind grain. Today the mill, the oldest structure of its kind still standing in Durham County, is used to cut lumber. As well, from June to September it produces apple cider.

A visit inside the mill finds a woodworking shop on the second floor. Antique tools, old flour sacks and wooden beams give testament to the age of the building.

Inside the store can be found apple cider, homemade jams, cheese, baked goods and a variety of other delicious items for sale.

This interesting spot can be visited year round Monday to Saturday from 9 a.m. to 6 p.m. and in summer from 1 to 5 p.m. on Sundays.

Marg, Bruce and I enjoyed our visit very much and we look forward to returning with the grandchildren to show them another bit of provincial history.

Sunday January 25

I shall light a candle of understanding in thy heart which shall not be put out.

2 Esdras 14:25, The Apocrypha

Monday January 26

I went shopping today with my granddaughter Phyllis as she outfitted her twins Jenny and Justin with new shoes. I must admit that I find the cost of shoes today to be flabbergasting—running shoes at nearly one hundred dollars a pair simply astound me.

As I sat with Phyllis and watched the salesman fit the shoes to the twins' feet I remembered something that I had long forgotten—the fluoroscope. At one time, in the early 1950s, everyone wanted to buy their shoes at a store equipped with one of these "miraculous" machines.

After putting a new pair of shoes on his or her feet, the child would then step onto the machine and place his or her feet in the fluoroscope. When turned on, the machine showed the bones of the foot surrounded by a blue light. Three people could be watching at once (through individual viewers) while the salesman operated a wand to point out interesting features of the shoe's fit.

I don't remember when or why this machine went out of favour, but I do recall many a child wanting a new pair of shoes just so that he or she could try out this amazing and fascinating machine.

Tuesday January 27

Our days are identical suitcases—all the same size—but some people can pack more into them than others.

Wednesday January 28

When you were born, you cried and the world rejoiced. Live your life in such a manner that when you die the world cries and you rejoice.

Indian proverb

Thursday January 29

The way a crow
Shook down on me
The dust of snow
From a hemlock tree

Has given my heart
A change of mood
And saved some part
Of a day I had rued.

Robert Frost

Friday January 30

My friends Will and Muriel came by today and Muriel was using crutches and sporting a cast on her ankle.

She explained, "I don't think I have ever felt more foolish, Edna. We had forgotten to put out the garbage and hearing the truck jogged my memory. I was in such a rush, hoping not to miss the pick-up, that I threw a coat on over my nightgown and set off down the driveway wearing only my slippers on my feet. The next thing I knew I was sliding down the icy drive like an out-of-control skier. As my feet hit the sanded sidewalk I came to a sudden stop where I went down in a heap, up to my ears in garbage.

"When they could finally control their laughter, the garbage men hurried to help me and call the ambulance. I won't do that again in a hurry!"

Saturday January 31

Worry is interest paid on trouble before it is due.

February

Sunday February 1

Who can number the sand of the sea, and the drops of rain, and the days of eternity?

Ecclesiasticus 1:2, The Apocrypha

Monday February 2

Today is Groundhog Day and, if you believe in superstition, you will know whether or not to expect six more weeks of winter weather.

How this particular notion got started I am not sure, but if Wiarton Willie or Punxsutawney Phil come out of their holes in Wiarton, Ontario, and Punxsutawney, Pennsylvania, and see their shadows they will return to their underground homes and we won't see spring for six more weeks. The idea that groundhogs could be weather forecasters seems odd but their predictions have been uncannily accurate.

I, for one, am hoping for a cloudy day. I am ready for Spring!

Tuesday February 3

Have you ever stood outside on a cold February evening and watched the stars come out? If you have, you will appreciate Sara Teasdale's poem "February Twilight."

I stood beside a hill
    Smooth with new-laid snow,
A single star looked out
    From the cold evening glow.

There was no other creature
    That saw what I could see—
I stood and watched the evening star
    As long as it watched me.

Wednesday February 4

Every one must have felt that a cheerful friend is like a sunny day, which sheds its brightness on all around; and most of us can, as we choose, make of this world a palace or a prison.

Sir John Lubbock

Thursday February 5

I received a letter from my dear friend Mavis Tewbury, a long-time resident of Manitoba. Although the times that we get together are few, we have maintained a close friendship through cards, letters and infrequent phone calls (reserved for momentous occasions such as the birth of a new grandchild).

Mavis is one of those people with a rare talent. She is able to write a letter exactly as if she were speaking directly to you. As I read her missive I can hear her voice in my head with every inflection and expression as clear as a bell.

Often when writing, people use a rather stilted language not at all in their normal pattern of speech. Not so with Mavis. All of her oft-used favourite expressions are right there to be enjoyed just as if she were in the chair beside you enjoying a chin-wag over coffee.

How I envy her this gift!

Friday February 6

Friendship is the inexpressible comfort of feeling safe with a person having neither to weigh thoughts nor measure words.

George Eliot

Saturday February 7

Many of my older friends often lament the passing of the "good old days." Although there is much to miss from those bygone days there is more to enjoy in our modern world.

For example, I can remember as a youngster sleeping under a load of blankets and wearing a hat to bed. Heat came only from a wood stove or the fireplace, and heavy clothes were worn indoors all the winter long.

Preparation for winter began in the previous summer. Vegetable gardens needed to be planted, then watered and weeded daily so that we would have enough canned food to see us through the long winter.

On many farms home butchering would provide the meat. Certain cuts of pork would be packed in large crocks of lard which were stored in the cellar.

In the smokehouse, hams were hung and cured over a hardwood fire.

Nothing was ever wasted. Hog fat was made into lard and stored in crocks for baking. Hog grease mixed with lye made laundry soap.

Keeping fruits and vegetables fresh was interesting. In early fall when they were ripe the cellar was too warm to store them. Instead, a hole was dug out back about a foot deep, filled with straw, then filled with fruits and vegetables—then covered with more straw, then dirt. When winter was near they were unburied and moved to the now cool cellar.

The good old days? I don't think so.

Sunday February 8

Ye are the light of the world. A city that is set on a hill cannot be hid. Neither do men light a candle, and put it under a bushel, but on a candlestick; and it giveth light unto all that are in the house.

Matthew 5:14–15

Monday February 9

If you want to see both complete innocence and the mystery of the ages, look into the eyes of a baby.

Bern Williams

Tuesday February 10

You have to count on living every single day in a way you believe will make you feel good about your life—so that if it were over tomorrow, you'd be content with yourself.

Seymour

Wednesday February 11

For two weeks this month the eyes of the world will be fixed on Nagano, Japan, site of the Winter Olympics. Athletes from hundreds of countries including Canada will compete in many disciplines, hoping to win a medal that will recognize them as one of the world's finest competitors.

The three top-ranking competitors in each event receive medals in recognition of their efforts.

First place is rewarded with a silver-gilt medal, known as gold, second with a silver medal and third with a bronze.

The medals themselves usually change very little from the design created for the 1928 Amsterdam games. The predominant symbols are victory, brotherhood and universality. The only changes are the numeric sequence of the Olympiad, the name of the host city and the date. The reverse often carries a symbol of the discipline for which the medal was received.

As ever, these three words are symbolic of Olympian efforts: *Citius, Altius, Fortius*—Faster, Higher, Stronger.

I wish much success to our Canadian athletes.

Thursday February 12

As I watched the children at play outdoors today I marvelled at their clothing. In spite of the frigid weather the children are warm and comfortable in brightly coloured lightweight snow-suits, hats, mittens and boots. Through the development of man-made fibres even thin, single-layer materials provide great warmth.

It used to be that children were bundled up in layer upon layer of clothing—long underwear, heavy slacks, flannel shirts, thick woollen socks and sweaters. On top of these were worn snow pants, a quilted jacket, thick woollen mittens and hats and bulky "grandma-knit" scarves wrapped around the face such that only the eyes were visible.

Often children were so heavily padded that their arms stood straight out and they waddled like ducks. Falling down could be disastrous, as it was often impossible to get up without help from an equally padded playmate.

To see the children so well occupied today and having so little difficulty moving around made me appreciate once again the incredible genius of the scientists who have developed the amazing warm and light fabrics that we take for granted.

Friday February 13

Those people who suffer from triskaidekapho-bia will be hiding indoors today. For those of you unfamiliar with this particular phobia, it is the fear of the number 13 and especially when it falls on a Friday.

For me, any day that I wake up feeling well and happy is a lucky day and I hope to enjoy it to the fullest.

Saturday February 14

ST. VALENTINE'S DAY

These lines from Sara Teasdale are, to me, perfect for Valentine's Day.

They came to tell your faults to me,
They named them over one by one;
I laughed aloud when they were done,
I knew them all so well before—
Oh, they were blind, too blind to see
Your faults had made me love you more.

Sunday February 15

God is our refuge and strength, a very present help in trouble.

Therefore will we not fear, though the earth be removed, and though the mountains be carried into the midst of the sea.

Psalms 46:1–2

Monday February 16

During a severe snowstorm in 1996 I talked to my friend Marcia, a resident of Boston, Massachusetts.

Marcia reported that she and her family had been marooned in their home for several days.

When I asked how her food supply was holding out, she replied, "Well we're not down to the licklog yet."

I hadn't heard that expression for years. A licklog was a grooved log in which the indentations were filled with salt for livestock. When the salt was gone, farmers said animals were down to the licklog.

Fortunately the weather improved and Marcia was able to replenish her larder before needing the "licklog."

Tuesday February 17

As my former readers know, our family members are lovers of books. As youngsters my brother, my sister and I were greatly encouraged by both of our parents to read all manner of literature from newspapers to poetry, novels and the classics. In turn we encouraged our children and grandchildren in this pursuit.

Others have written of this love, and I offer some of their thoughts today.

Books are the true levellers. They give to all, pleasure.

Noah Porter

The use of books for pleasure is the most satisfactory recreation; without having acquired the power of reading for pleasure, none of us can be independent.

Viscount Grey

Literature is my utopia.

Helen Keller

I cannot live without books.

Thomas Jefferson

Wednesday February 18

Swedish film director Ingmar Bergman had this interesting observation on old age:

It's like climbing a mountain. You climb from ledge to ledge. The higher you get, the more tired and breathless you become, but your view becomes much more extensive.

Thursday February 19

Charm has a magical quality that defrosts, disarms, delights and fascinates. It is not a sudden gush of sweetness that can be turned off and on like a faucet. It is woven subtly into the fabric of the personality, like a silver thread. It glistens. It shines. It wears well.

Ann Landers

Friday February 20

Coming together is a beginning; keeping together is progress; working together is success.

Henry Ford

Saturday February 21

My sister Sarah and her husband Richard celebrate their sixth wedding anniversary tomorrow.

What a wonderful relationship they enjoy. Although they were friends for many years their friendship didn't blossom into a romance for a very long time. As Sarah puts it, "We just sort of 'evolved.' We went to church together Sunday mornings, we enjoyed dinner quite regularly at each other's homes and we spent many many evenings just talking over tea. Then, more often, Richard brought flowers or other small gifts or he would add candles to our dinner table. Soon we realized that we wanted to spend all of the time remaining to us together."

In 1992, with many friends and family with them to share in their happy day, Richard and Sarah were married.

Their happiness continues and I wish them many many more years of joy together.

The thread of our life would be dark, heaven knows!

If it were not with friendship and love intertwin'd.

Thomas Moore

Sunday February 22

Father, I have much to be grateful for tonight, and I thank you. I have much to regret and I ask your forgiveness. But even as I ask your forgiveness, I know that I receive it, and a deep peace fills my heart.

Help me to sleep well tonight and to wake ready for that daily yet greatest of gifts, a fresh start.

Avery Brooke

Monday February 23

Whenever a man's friends begin to compliment him about looking young, he may be sure that they think he is growing old.

Washington Irving

Tuesday February 24

My son-in-law John remarked from his bed, "Never be the last member in the family to get the flu. By then all the sympathy has run out."

Wednesday February 25

ASH WEDNESDAY

Lay up for yourselves treasures in heaven where neither moth nor rust doth corrupt, and where thieves do not break through nor steal; for where your treasure is, there will your heart be also.

Book of Common Prayer

Thursday February 26

I am quite fond of potpourri and over the years I have collected a number of recipes that are easy to make but which offer a very fragrant scent.

One of the easiest to produce for yourself (and friends) needs only two ingredients: orange peel and cloves.

My dear friend Emily, who winters in Florida, often sends a large bag of oranges to me and this is how I use them. You need 1 dozen oranges and 6 ounces of cloves. Collect the peel of a dozen oranges and break into pieces about 1 inch square. Insert 1 whole clove into each piece of peel. (Add 2 or 3 to each piece if you prefer a more pungent odour.)

Set the peel to dry in a flat basket or box.

When the peel is dry, scoop it into several small bowls or baskets to scent your room.

Add a ribbon to the basket and you have a gift for a friend.

Friday February 27

The sound of laughter has always seemed to me to be the most civilized music in the universe.

Peter Ustinov

Saturday February 28

I enjoy the many winter birds that come to my feeder during cold weather. Chickadees, cardinals, blue jays and others are a cheery, and usually noisy, addition to the winterscape of our yard.

In our westernmost province of British Columbia the bald eagle is a common winter visitor. These birds migrate from the northernmost part of their range. Because bald eagles live largely on fish, the high evergreens of the Gulf Islands provide the birds with excellent vantage points from which they can search for food.

The waters around the Gulf Islands and the Vancouver area are open, but sheltered, during winter. They provide a large selection of food for these magnificent birds—once nearly extinct but now becoming more plentiful, as they are a protected species.

They are certainly worth watching for on any winter visit to this area of our country.

March

Sunday March 1

Man shall not live by bread alone but by every word that proceedeth out of the mouth of God.

Matthew 4:4

Monday March 2

Although I enjoy most sports I confess that I have never cared for boxing. I did enjoy the story, however, that my friend Will related about former boxing great Rocky Graziano.

When Graziano was asked why he retired from the ring he replied, "I looked in the mirror after my last fight and saw my beaten-up face and decided there must be an easier way to meet congenial people of my own age."

Tuesday March 3

As my former readers know, I am an avid fan of the sport of figure skating. Whenever there is a competition or an exhibition on television I watch, enthralled.

Two of my favourite skaters were the members of the Russian pairs team, Ekaterina Gordeeva and Sergei Grinkov.

Both excellent individual skaters, they were paired up when Sergei was 15 and Katia (as she is called) was a tiny 11-year-old. They were immediately successful, winning many international events and reigning as the Junior World Champions in their first attempt. They were Olympic champions in Calgary in 1988.

Their partnership turned to love and they were married. A beautiful daughter, Daria, was born, and the young couple continued to skate, winning Olympic gold again in Albertville, France, in 1994.

Tragedy struck in November of 1995 as Sergei, only 28 years old, collapsed and died on the ice during a practice session in Lake Placid.

Katia was shattered and declared that she would never skate again. However, using the love and support of her skating friends and drawing strength from her delightful child, she gave a solo performance in Hartford, Connecticut, in February 1996—an exquisite tribute to her late husband.

She proves that life goes on!

Wednesday March 4

Treasure the love you receive above all. It will survive long after your gold and good health have vanished.

Og Mandino

Thursday March 5

Dag Hammarskjöld, at one time the president of the United Nations, died, too young, in a plane crash. After his death, this prophetic poem that Dag had translated as a young schoolboy was found in the family Bible.

The day you were born everybody was happy—
  you cried alone.
Make your life such that in your last hour all
  others are weeping,
And you are the only one without a tear to shed!
Then you shall calmly face death, whenever it
  comes.

Friday March 6

So long as we love, we serve. So long as we are loved by others we are indispensable; and no man is useless while he has a friend.

Robert Louis Stevenson

Saturday March 7

My daughter Julia and I spent much of this day enjoying the many and varied works of art at a local art museum.

I readily confess that my taste in art is rather primitive. If the artist has labelled his painting "Rider on Horseback," that is exactly what I expect to see. The more the picture looks like a photograph, the better I like it!

Julia, on the other hand, is able to appreciate art in its many forms. She sees subtle nuances in paintings that I am not able to comprehend.

Several years ago Julia was lucky enough to be in Paris during the time of an exhibition of works by the renowned French artist Henri Matisse.

Matisse is widely known for his bold use of primary colour, and his most famous works depict dance and music. However, the drawings in Visages Découverts (Faces Uncovered) were done between 1945 and 1954 when he was forced, by declining health, to use charcoal, pencils and pastels to draw.

Hidden from the public for decades, 135 portraits, aquatints and lithographs, including dozens of his beloved grandchildren Claude, Jackie and Gerrard, were a part of the exhibit at the Mona Bismark Foundation in Paris.

Julia was thrilled to be able to see the works of a true master.

Sunday March 8

Almighty God, who seest that we have no power of ourselves to keep ourselves: Keep us both outwardly in our bodies and inwardly in our souls; that we may be defended from all adversities which may happen to the body, and from all evil which may assault and hurt the soul; through Jesus Christ our Lord. Amen.

The Book of Common Prayer

Monday March 9

My son-in-law John, a minister, appreciated this story very much. It was a part of a speech given by then President of the United States Ronald Reagan.

A farmer took a piece of bad earth and made things flourish thereon. Proud of his accomplishments, he asked his minister to come by and see what he'd done. The minister was impressed. "That's the tallest corn I've ever seen! And those melons—bigger than anything I've seen. Praise the Lord!"

He continued to exclaim over every crop, praising the Lord for all of it.

Finally the farmer could stand no more. "Reverend," he said, "I wish you could have seen this place when the Lord was doing it by himself."

Tuesday March 10

The Moon of March comes roughly riding in,
Spring sitting on its shoulders like a child;
With frisky lambs, unseasonably mild,
And roaring lions with their cubs and kin.

March has the wit to lose, the wit to win,
With north and south winds hardly reconciled;
But in the bush the maple sticks are piled,
Ready to help the sugaring begin.

A month of contradictions: snowdrops rise
To find their bloom betrayed by colder snow.
The early robin takes us by surprise
To shiver in a storm's unkindly blow;
But then the shamrock, lovely to the eyes,
Greenly reminds us Winter has to go.

My special thanks go to the author of this poem,
Hume Wilkins. This work is from his book *Every
Day Is A Gift*.

Mr. Wilkins published his book as a way of
thanking the health-givers who kept him well, and
in particular Dr. Ted Kryn, Dr. T.E. Hodgins and
the staff of physicians, surgeons, nurses and aux-
iliary staff who helped him during his stay at the
Kitchener-Waterloo hospital in 1983.

Proceeds from the sale of his book are donated
to buy books for the libraries of the Plattsville
schools.

Wednesday March 11

What parents leave in their children is much more important than what they leave to them.

Thursday March 12

When a man's pursuit gradually makes his face shine and grow handsome, be sure it is a worthy one.

William James

Friday March 13

Henry Ford, the American auto genius, was an expert at time management. When asked why he rarely summoned executives to his office to sort out problems, he replied, "I go to them to save time. I've found that I can leave the other fellow's office a lot quicker than I can get him to leave mine."

Saturday March 14

My husband George was keenly interested in the aboriginals of our country. I know that he would have enjoyed our family outing today.

Just south of the town of Campbellville is the Crawford Lake Conservation Area. The area boasts 12 kilometres of rugged but groomed trails for skiing and hiking. The trails wind through the quiet woods and along the cliffs of the Niagara Escarpment. From an elevated boardwalk you can see Crawford Lake, a rare geological find. Corn pollen excavated from successive layers of the lake's sediment has helped archeologists to date the occupation of the Iroquois to between 1200 and 1645 A.D.

My great-grandchildren, Justin and Jenny, were particularly interested in the reconstructed 15th-century Iroquois log house. Looking at the skins on the wooden bunks and the other artifacts made it easy to imagine life in the times long ago.

The Wolf Clan Longhouse has a mini-theatre, an archeology exhibit and a display of the daily life of the native people.

The children also enjoyed learning about the games played by Indian children as explained at the interpretive stations in the village.

This is a wonderful outing for all ages.

Sunday March 15

And I say unto you, Ask, and it shall be given you; seek, and ye shall find; knock, and it shall be opened unto you.

For everyone that asketh receiveth; and he that seeketh findeth; and to him that knocketh it shall be opened.

Luke 11: 9–10

Monday March 16

I continue to be amazed by the advances made in science and technology. At dinner this evening Bruce read to us an article that described other possible changes that could occur after the turn of the century.

Cars will drive themselves. With the aid of computers you will select your destination and relax until you get there.

Cash will disappear. People will use "smart cards" similar to today's bank cards. These cards will also store medical data, credit balances and other information.

High-tech schooling will begin in infancy with special equipment adapted to the crib. Babies will play electronic games and learn to read by age 3.

For someone like me who still has difficulty understanding how a plane flies or a television works, these concepts are overwhelming!

Tuesday March 17

ST. PATRICK'S DAY

Those of you who are Irish probably know of the history of St. Patrick, known as the "Apostle of Ireland." To you who may be unaware, I offer this bit of interesting information.

St. Patrick's birthplace is uncertain but is thought to be in southwestern Britain. At age 16 he was kidnapped by Irish invaders and taken to Ireland, where he spent his captivity as a herdsman in County Antrim (as tradition avers) or in County Connacht. There he saw visions that urged him to escape, and after six years of slavery he did so, fleeing to France. In France he was ordained as a priest. He returned to Ireland and was appointed bishop, Ireland's second, sometime after 431. It is believed that because he used the shamrock to illustrate the mystery of the Trinity, the Irish grew to regard it as their national symbol.

Today, a celebration of this day includes the "wearin' o' the green" and the serving of green food and drink.

To all of you who claim Irish heritage I wish you a Happy St. Patrick's Day!

Wednesday March 18

Nothing in life is more wonderful than faith—the one great moving force which we can neither weigh in the balance nor test in the crucible.

Sir William Osler

Thursday March 19

The age of a person doesn't mean a thing. The best music is played on the oldest violins.

Friday March 20

Pioneer Catharine Parr Traill describes a sugaring-off scene in her journal, *The Backwoods of Canada*. "It was a pretty and picturesque sight to see the sugar-boilers, with their bright log-fire among the trees, now stirring up the blazing pile, now throwing in the liquid and stirring it down with a big ladle. When the fire grew fierce, it boiled and foamed up in the kettle, and they had to throw in fresh sap to keep it from running over."

How little this has changed over the years.

Saturday March 21

This day is a double celebration in our family. It is not only the first day of spring but also the birthday of my great-granddaughter Bethany.

This child has been a great joy to us all from the day she was born. Her wonderful sunny disposition is a "pick-me-up" for everyone, young or old.

Blessed be childhood, which brings down something of heaven into the midst of our rough earthliness.

Henri Frédéric Amiel

Sunday March 22

No man, when he hath lighted a candle, putteth it in a secret place, neither under a bushel, but on a candlestick, that they which come in may see the light.

Luke 11:33

Monday March 23

"I must do something" will always solve more problems than "Something must be done."

Tuesday March 24

Spring brings thoughts of flowers. My friend Will is always a great help in assisting us with the selection of the flowers for our garden.

During their visit today Will and his wife Muriel read to me a most interesting article about flowers and personalities.

If the rose is your favourite, you are a person who expects the best. The thorns make roses hard to handle and they prove that you don't mind working hard to surround yourself with lovely things.

The carnation, a traditional bloom, shows that you prefer basic things if this is your flower of choice. For you, things don't have to be the biggest and the best to be worthwhile.

If you love daisies, your taste is for dainty, delicate things.

Orchid fanciers enjoy exotic and expensive things. Orchids don't last long, so you believe in seizing the moment.

You who choose the lily as your favourite like to make your presence felt. Lilies are stately and dignified and so are you.

Tulips are not usually mixed with other types of flowers; this shows you are an individualist.

Will and Muriel have decided that I must have a very odd personality as I love them all!

Wednesday March 25

My beloved friend Lila MacGuiness has been in the hospital. Although she hopes to be home soon, this has not been an easy time for her. I hope that Lila can use this prayer to bring some comfort.

Today, Lord, I feel lonely and alone.

It is difficult to lie quietly on this bed in silent mediation.

Answers to my prayers seem long in coming, and to trust you without questioning is not easy.

You have cared for me before; now please care for me again!

In my aloneness and my loneliness grant me your presence and your help. Then I will know that I can lie down and sleep in peace.

Because you hear my prayer you have mercy on me and you keep me safe!

Thursday March 26

Our neighbour, John, remarked that arguing with his wife Lynn is like "trying to blow out an electric light bulb."

Friday March 27

As the hockey season draws to a close the play-offs are just around the corner. My husband George and I loved to spend an evening with the girls listening to the games on the radio or, in later years, watching them on television.

One of the most amazing playoff games in history took place in Montreal in 1928. At the time Lester Patrick was the silver-haired coach and manager of the New York Rangers. The Rangers were playing the second game of a best of three series against the Montreal Maroons. Early in the second period, Ranger goalie Lorne Chabot suffered a severe eye injury and was taken to hospital. In those days, teams had no back-up goaltender.

Patrick donned the pads and proceeded to put on an inspirational performance for the final half of the game in spite of the fact that he had never before played goal.

His outstanding play revived his underdog team and they went on to win the game 2–1, knotting the series at a game apiece.

It was a game that would be long remembered!

Saturday March 28

A moment's insight is sometimes worth a life's experience.

Oliver Wendell Holmes

Sunday March 29

These things I have spoken unto you that in me you might have peace. In the world you shall have troubles: but be happy; I have overcome the world.

John 16:33

Monday March 30

The aim of education is to teach us how to think, not what to think.

Tuesday March 31

Joy is a net of love by which you catch souls.

Mother Teresa

April

Wednesday April 1

For every sunset there's a sunrise,
For every winter comes a spring,
For every word in anger spoken
There's joy and gladness kind words bring.

For every raindrop there's a sunbeam,
For every tear a lovely smile,
For every storm a promise given—
This too shall pass in just awhile.

Life's made of contrasts, sweet and bitter
Into each life they both must fall;
But, be it trial or be it blessing
We know God's hand is in it all.

If life were always bright and happy
Would we seek help from above
Or know the joy when breaks the morning
With rainbowed skies of hope and love?

My thanks to the unknown author for today's
words.

Thursday April 2

I am grateful for the spring-like weather of recent days. As I grow older I find winter weather less and less to my liking. I know I am not alone in this because so many of my elderly friends have chosen to spend as long as six months of the year enjoying the sunny climes of Florida, Texas, Arizona or California.

Don and Emily, good friends from New Brunswick, spent a large part of this winter in the area of San Antonio, Texas. There is much to see in this historic part of the United States.

The Alamo, known as the cradle of Texas liberty, was built originally as a part of Mission San Antonio de Valero. After 1740 a chapel was added, and later the compound became a fort. In February of 1836, during the Texas Revolution, more than 4,000 Mexican troops led by General Santa Anna laid siege to the site, which was defended by some 188 men. The forces, including James Bowie and Davy Crockett, refused to surrender and fought to their deaths. In later years the rallying cry in Texas became "Remember the Alamo!"

Other areas of interest are the San Antonio Museum of Art, The Hertzberg Circus and Museum, featuring a variety of items belonging to P.J. Barnum, and the Paseo del Rio, the River Walk through the heart of the downtown district.

Friday April 3

Babies haven't any hair,
Old men's heads are just as bare;
Between the cradle and the grave
Lies a haircut and a shave.

My son-in-law, Bruce, is now quite bald, as were his father and grandfather before him. According to Bruce, the earliest recorded baldness remedy dates back to 4000 B.C. when the mother of King Chata of Egypt recommended rubbing the balding head with a mixture of ground-up dog's paws, dates and ass's hooves cooked in oil. Since that time, men, desperate to stop the inevitable, have worked with all manner of bizarre lotions and potions.

Over the years Bruce has heard all kinds of strange ideas. Some people thought that you could save your hair if you ate parsnips every day, cut your hair only on the first Friday of the full moon, rinsed your hair in salt water or poured rum on your head.

Suggested methods of hair restoration included smearing the bald spot with cow manure, rubbing the bald spot daily with a mixture of axle grease and cod liver oil, or (my particular favourite) spreading cream on the bald spot and letting the cat lick it off.

Bruce has decided that "Bald is Beautiful" and he needs no more suggested "cures." I believe he is right!

Saturday April 4

If you would have your son be something in the world, teach him to depend upon himself. Let him learn that it is by close and strenuous personal application he must rise—that he must, in short, make himself, and be architect of his own fortune.

Howard Edwards

Sunday April 5

PALM SUNDAY

For all flesh is as grass, and all the glory of man as the flower of grass. The grass withereth, and the flower thereof falleth away:

But the word of the Lord endureth forever. And this is the word which by the gospel is preached unto you.

1 Peter 1: 24–25

Monday April 6

"Stay" is a charming word in a friend's vocabulary.

Louisa May Alcott

Tuesday April 7

We are at the beginning of the baseball season and I look forward to a great season for "my boys," the Toronto Blue Jays.

One of the most interesting men ever to be involved in the game of baseball was the great New York Yankee manager Casey Stengel. An astute and clever manager, he seemed able to get the best from all of his players.

After the expansion of the league Stengel found himself managing the New York Mets, one of the most hapless groups of players ever to play pro ball.

At one point Stengel was quoted as saying, "Can't anyone here play this game?"

In 1975 Stengel, who was by then 85 years old, went to Glendale Memorial Hospital "for a checkup." He was, in fact, terminally ill with cancer.

He lay in bed watching a baseball game on television. As the national anthem was being played before the game, he was heard to say, "I might as well do this one last time." He swung his legs over the side of the bed, got to his feet and stood at attention with his hand over his heart.

On September 29, the day after the baseball season ended, Casey Stengel died and the game lost a legend.

Wednesday April 8

The winter is past, the rain is over and gone; The flowers appear on the earth; the time of the singing of birds is come.

Song of Solomon 2:11–12

Thursday April 9

The first hour of the morning is the rudder of the day.

Henry Ward Beecher

Friday April 10

GOOD FRIDAY

Good Friday marks the most difficult of days for Jesus. He is guiltless and yet he is crucified—a tragedy that is hard for his followers to accept. The soldiers mock him: "If thou be the king of the Jews, save thyself."

And yet, when his suffering is almost unbearable, he utters a ten-word prayer that will ring out forevermore: "Father, forgive them, for they know not what they do."

Saturday April 11

It is always darkest just before the day dawneth.

Thomas Fuller

Sunday April 12

EASTER SUNDAY

When my husband George was alive, Easter was the day of the year that he most enjoyed. It was the day that was the true basis of his faith. Jesus' death and rise to the glory of heaven always gave him a great sense of renewal.

"He was dead and is alive again." This is the victory that we Christians share on Easter, Christ's victory over death.

Alleluia! Alleluia! Like the sun from out the wave
He has risen up in triumph
From the darkness of the grave;
He's the splendour of the nation
He's the lamp of endless day
He's the very Lord of glory
Who has risen up today.

Book of Common Prayer

Monday April 13

My daughter Mary and her husband John stayed with me this weekend. John is a minister and their life together closely parallels the life that George and I experienced. John's stories of parish life are always of great interest and make me a little nostalgic for those long-ago years.

One of John's younger parish couples taught their three-year-old daughter to say grace before meals. Then one day her mother, who was washing the baby in the sink as Emily was taking her bath, heard her carefully reciting the prayer.

"Sweetheart, this isn't the time to say grace," said her mother. "You do that just before you eat."

"I know," she answered, quite cheerfully, "but I just swallowed the soap."

Tuesday April 14

Each day is a gift and a cause for celebrating who we are, what we have achieved and all the joy we have yet to know.

Wednesday April 15

Knowledge has never been known to enter the head via an open mouth.

Doug Larsen

Thursday April 16

Luciano Pavarotti, one of the finest tenors the world has ever known, became a singer with the help and advice of his father. Pavarotti has told this story many times, but his father's advice would be helpful for us all.

When Pavarotti was a boy his father, a baker, introduced him to the wonders of music. He urged his son to develop his voice, and so Luciano became a pupil of Arrigo Pola, a professional tenor in his home town of Modessa, Italy. He also enrolled in a teacher's college. After graduating he asked his father, "Shall I be a teacher or a singer?"

His father answered, "Luciano, if you try to sit on two chairs, you will fall between them. For life, you must choose one chair."

Luciano chose music. It was seven years before he made his first professional appearance and seven more before he performed at the Metropolitan Opera.

His advice to others now? "Whatever we choose—we should give ourselves to it. Commitment is the key. Choose one chair."

Friday April 17

As I walked through our neighbourhood today it was a joy to see the signs of spring. Blossoms, flowers, birds—all are showing themselves to the warmer sun. I was reminded of these lines by James Russell Lowell and they seemed to fit today perfectly.

We sit in the warm shade and feel right well
How the sap creeps up and the blossoms swell;
We may shut our eyes, but we cannot help
      knowing
That skies are clear and grass is growing;
The breeze comes whispering in our ear;
That dandelions are blossoming near,
That maize has sprouted, that streams are
      flowing,
That the river is bluer than the sky,
That the robin is plastering his house nearby....

Saturday April 18

The best way to succeed in life is to act on the advice you give to others.

Sunday April 19

Whatsoever is born of God overcometh the world: and this is the victory that overcometh the world, even our faith.

1 John 5:4

Monday April 20

My brother Ben is an avid gardener so he welcomes the month of April with joy.

As his wife Marie explains, "Ben is never happier than when he is working in his garden. He spends the winter cleaning and oiling his tools. Sometimes he'll just go down to the basement and 'make sure that the tools are in order.' I'm not sure if that means that they are neat or in an alphabetical arrangement. You know me, Edna; lawns, trees, flowers are all beautiful and I love them—so long as there's somebody else around to take care of them. For me gardens are to read in (or nap in on a lazier day). Thank goodness for your brother. We have the loveliest garden in our neighbourhood but it is no thanks to me at all. 'April showers bring May Flowers' but first it brings Ben in the garden."

Tuesday April 21

"Call 911!" This lifesaving phone number is being used more and more all across North America.

As I'm sure you remember, each city, town and rural area used to have individual phone numbers for all emergencies. Police, hospitals, ambulances, fire departments, etc. had different numbers, and getting in touch with the right people, particularly in a stressful situation, could often take considerable time.

I believe that California was the first area to test 911. Operators, trained in emergency response, would take the name, address and nature of the emergency and, keeping the caller on the line, would "patch through" to the correct response team. The results were spectacular, to say the least. Many lives that might otherwise have been lost were being saved by the quick response time to the emergency situations.

Children as young as two or three years of age have dialled the 911 help lines and have received immediate assistance.

Rescue 911 has been one of the most popular television shows ever made, citing true stories of the help line's use.

If an emergency arises I hope that you are lucky enough to be in a 911 area!

Wednesday April 22

Marg suggested earlier today that it could be time to begin the annual "pre-summer diet." Each year Bruce is less and less enthusiastic about this regimen, but tonight he had us laughing as he came to dinner armed with these words from Washington Irving:

Who ever heard of fat men heading a riot, or herding together in turbulent mobs?—no—no 'tis your lean, hungry men who are continually worrying society, and setting the whole community by the ears.

"Now Marg, I need to eat so I needn't lead a riot!"

Thursday April 23

I am bigger than anything that can happen to me. All these things, sorrow, misfortune and suffering, are outside my door. I am in the house and I have the key.

Charles Fletcher Lummis

Friday April 24

A man travels the world over in search of what he needs and returns home to find it.

Saturday April 25

This is the time of year that university graduation ceremonies take place. All across the country proud graduates, watched by even prouder parents, are receiving their diplomas, a reward for years of hard work.

Our great Canadian humourist Stephen Leacock liked to poke fun at these institutes of higher learning when he felt that they were taking themselves just a little too seriously. In "Oxford as I See It" he wrote:

If I were founding a university I would found first a smoking room; then when I had a little more money in hand I would found a dormitory; then after that, or more probably with it, a decent reading room and a library. After that, if I still had more money that I couldn't use, I would hire a professor and get some textbooks.

Sunday April 26

Jesus said, "I am the good shepherd: the good shepherd giveth his life for the sheep.

John 10:11

Monday April 27

The person who says it can't be done should not interrupt the person doing it.

Chinese proverb

Tuesday April 28

My grandson Marshall enjoys playing golf and tries to play as often as he can. Although the courses in our area are not yet open, he was able to enjoy several matches when he was in South Carolina for a few days. When I asked how his game was, he laughed and said, "It wasn't too bad, Gran, except that we followed two real slowpokes."

On the fifteenth fairway one of the men was in his golf cart reading a book. His partner was thrashing about in the deep rough while Marshall and his friend waited.

"Don't you think you should help your partner find his ball?" asked Marshall.

"Oh, he's got his ball," drawled the reader. "He's lookin' for his club."

Wednesday April 29

A cheerful friend is like a sunny day.

Thursday April 30

Although I am barely "computer literate," I am fascinated by how this marvellous technology can be of benefit in so many ways. My friend Jake recounted this interesting story to me this evening.

A few years ago Scottish detective Constable Jim McNulty reported online that a London officer had been killed and two others injured in the line of duty. Officers from other countries around the world wondered why bulletproof vests had not worked. Constable McNulty explained that the government of Great Britain doesn't supply the vests to its officers and many of the men found them too expensive to buy for themselves.

A Las Vegas policeman, Lieutenant Dennis Cobb, responded by E-mail offering his spare vest. Within days officers all across Canada and the U.S. offered vests that were due to be replaced but were still effective.

Within a few weeks more than 1,500 vests had been sent to Britain, with Virgin Atlantic Airways shipping them free of charge from Boston's Logan Airport to Heathrow in London.

Constable McNulty was astonished at the response of his fellow officers worldwide.

I am astonished at the technology that provided the response.

May

Friday May 1

This traditional English poem, "The Mayers' Song," is a welcome to the beautiful month of May.

We've been a-rambling all this night
And sometime of this day;
And now returning back again
We bring a branch of May.

A branch of May we bring you here,
And at your door it stands;
It is but a sprout well budded out,
The work of our Lord's hands.

The hedges and trees they are so green,
As green as any leek;
Our heavenly Father, He watered them
With his heavenly dew so sweet.

The moon shines bright, the stars give a light
A little before it is day,
So God bless you all, both great and small,
And send you a joyful May.

Saturday May 2

Have you noticed that old age is always ten years older than you are?

Sunday May 3

And ye now therefore have sorrow: but I will see you again, and your heart shall rejoice, and your joy no man taketh from you.

John 16:22

Monday May 4

My daughter Julia does a lot of travelling in her job. Although much of her travel is done by plane to faraway countries of the world, there are other times when she drives to her destination.

One evening last week her meetings ran very late and it was after midnight when she set off for home.

"I knew that I was tired, but it was just a few hours to home and I really thought that I could make it safely.

"The oncoming lights seemed to hypnotize me, and about an hour into my drive I nodded off. It was just for a moment and I woke up just before I hit a metal guardrail. That terrified me!

"I quickly pulled off at the next exit and checked into a motel. I can't believe that I wasn't smart enough to realize how tired I was. I will *never* drive when I am that fatigued again."

I hope other drivers are as wise as Julia!

Tuesday May 5

One of the most difficult things to open is a closed mind.

Wednesday May 6

My grandson Marshall and his wife Jamie brought their children over for dinner this evening.

Bethany, a six-year-old, is a happy little girl who is content to sit quietly and play or read and amuse herself for hours.

Michael, at two-and-a-half, is giving new meaning to the expression "terrible twos." He is mobile, excitable and into everything. As Jamie puts it, "If he were twins I would probably be a crazy person by now."

I confess that it makes me very pleased to see how well these young people are raising their children. Both Jamie and Marshall have incredible patience and they discipline the youngsters with loving kindness. That is so important if children are to grow to be well-adjusted and kind adults.

I know that my husband George would have been so proud of his family.

Thursday May 7

Where there is charity and wisdom, there is neither fear nor ignorance. Where there is patience and humility, there is neither anger nor vexation. Where there is poverty and joy, there is neither greed nor avarice. Where there is peace and meditation, there is neither anxiety nor doubt.

St. Francis of Assisi

Friday May 8

The works of artist Vincent Van Gogh are some of the world's loveliest. "The Sunflowers" and "The Potato Eaters" are two of my favourites, but he produced about 700 drawings and 800 oils in his lifetime.

What is worth remembering about Van Gogh is that he is said to have sold but *one* painting while he lived.

Recognition of his talent came only after his death.

If you are questioning your own progress, you would do well to remember that the world sometimes takes a long time to recognize a talent.

Saturday May 9

The fact that something is beyond our vision doesn't mean it isn't there.

Sunday May 10

MOTHER'S DAY

I have always enjoyed the poetry of Edna St. Vincent Millay, and this poem to celebrate Mother's Day is a particular favourite.

The courage that my mother had
Went with her, and is with her still:
Rock from New England quarried;
Now granite in a granite hill.

The golden brooch my mother wore
She left behind for me to wear;
I have no thing I treasure more:
Yet, it is something I could spare.

Oh, if instead she'd left to me
The thing she took into the grave!—
That courage like a rock, which
She has no more need of, and I have.

Monday May 11

Most of the shadows of life are caused by standing in our own sunshine.

Ralph Waldo Emerson

Tuesday May 12

Marg and I do volunteer work in our local primary school and we enjoy it very much.

I have heard people say that teachers have an easy job, working 8:45–3:30, or that they have too much vacation time. They could not be more wrong!

Almost without exception all members of the staff arrive before 8 a.m., and those teachers not involved in the early morning athletic practices are meeting with colleagues to discuss programming or organization of extra-curricular activities.

Through the day teachers have the responsibility of teaching a demanding curriculum to students whose abilities can vary as much as two or three grade levels in each class.

Add to this children who exhibit an ever-increasing array of behaviour problems, and I wonder how any teachers can possibly cope with the expectations that are placed upon them.

As well, there are after-school activities, meetings, marking and correcting of assignments and lesson planning that continues at home late into the evenings.

I would challenge those who consider teaching to be "easy" to try it for even a few days. I believe they would soon sing a different tune.

Wednesday May 13

A number of years ago my brother Ben underwent heart bypass surgery. The operation was very successful and Ben has since enjoyed good health and an active lifestyle.

Since the time that we learned of Ben's heart problem our family has become much more aware of the dangers of heart disease and how we can lower the risk of developing this life-threatening disease.

Start with diet: Cutting saturated fat and cholesterol intake is important. People whose "bad" cholesterol level is high may also need medication to lower it.

Exercise is extremely important. Walking, cycling or swimming for 30 minutes three times per week is a good start. Doctors will usually recommend a program of exercise to suit your needs.

Excess weight is another contributor to heart disease. Losing those extra pounds can also lower your blood pressure.

Reducing alcohol and salt consumption can be a benefit, but your doctor will recommend this if it is necessary.

Drugs play a vital role in preventing further coronary damage for those who have had previous problems.

Following your doctor's recommendations can save your life!

Thursday May 14

It may take you forever to win men's minds by persuasion, but that's quicker than you can do it by force.

Frank Clark

Friday May 15

My grandson Fred and his wife June enjoy an occasional visit to the racetrack. John likes to buy a program and pick the winners according to breeding or past performance. June, on the other hand, relies on her intuition and "the lovely colour of the eyes." Their success is pretty much equal.

Fred passed along this story from his reading.

In June 1945 at Santa Anita, California, Quick Reward stumbled and lost his rider but, recovering, headed instinctively for the rail and raced after the leading horses. He pounded down the stretch and at the wire just nosed in front to finish first.

Apparently no one had told the horse that losing the rider means an automatic disqualification. After crossing the finish line he pulled up and walked straight to the winner's circle.

Saturday May 16

This is the first long weekend of the cottage season and, as has been our custom for many years, we are in Muskoka. Since Eleanor's husband passed away many years ago, Marg, Bruce and I have headed north to help open the cottage and ready it for the summer to come. Since Eleanor's "cottage" is really more of a home, the opening is not an onerous task.

My job is to dust and polish the furniture and to vacuum throughout. Today's lightweight vacuums and "no rub" polish make this part of the cleanup a breeze!

I can remember many years ago when George and the girls and I offered to help some friends open their cottage. It was an experience!

We had to get there by boat, a cumbersome wooden boat with a large motor that was unable, or unwilling, to start.

"Oh well," said Neal, "we'll row across."

With George and Neal manning the oars, the rest of us sat huddled between bags of food and bedding. With each pull of the oars more water splashed into the boat, and soon we were a sodden mess.

The cottage roof leaked, the stove billowed smoke, the bedding never dried and most of the food was inedible.

We had a wonderful time!

Sunday May 17

These things I have spoken unto you, that in me ye might have peace. In the world ye shall have tribulation: but be of good cheer; I have overcome the world.

John 16:33

Monday May 18

How I love the cry of the loon! This morning as I lay in bed I awakened to haunting calls first from one side of the bay and then the other.

I slipped out of bed onto the porch where I sat and watched as the two birds performed their beautiful dance on the water. One bird cries and then raises its wings, seeming to stand on its tail, and flaps quickly, only to settle back down and float in silence. The second bird answers back with a slightly more shrill cry and a wing salute.

Then silently they dive under the water and when I see them again they are floating side by side, black beacons in the morning mist.

It is so beautiful it brings tears to my eyes.

Tuesday May 19

The traffic returning to the city last night was extremely heavy. As Bruce put it, "I don't think this is holiday Monday traffic. I think it's Friday drivers still looking for a place to park."

Wednesday May 20

We only see a little of the ocean,
A few miles distance from the rocky shore;
But oh! Out there beyond—beyond the eye's
    horizon,
There's more—there's more.
We only see a little of God's loving,
A few rich treasures from his mighty store
But oh! Out there beyond—beyond our life's
    horizon
There's more—there's more.

Author unknown

Thursday May 21

ASCENSION DAY

And when he had spoken these things, while they beheld, he was taken up; and a cloud received him out of their sight.

Acts 1:9

Friday May 22

A few years ago there was a most interesting study done at Harvard University. This study found that children who come from a loving home are healthier later in life.

Students who believed that their parents loved and cared about them were much healthier 35 years later than those who felt that the parenting that they received was wanting.

This study showed that subjects who felt that their parents were harsh or unloving showed higher incidence of heart disease, high blood pressure, alcoholism and other stress-related illnesses as they got older.

I have to say that the results of this study really didn't surprise me. If you think about it, do you not feel more comfortable within yourself when things are happy and running along smoothly? Stress from an argument or unhappy feelings is like a knot in my stomach. Surely this must affect one physically as well as mentally.

How important it must be, then, to help our children and our grandchildren to feel the love and security that we can give them. I'm sure it's never too late to start....

Saturday May 23

As the sun warms and temperatures rise, it is wise to remember how important it is to protect ourselves from the damaging rays of the sun.

Here in Canada we have "borrowed" the three-word sun code used in Australia: Slip, Slap, Slop.

Slip on a shirt,
Slap on a hat,
Slop on the sunscreen.

Although this is good advice for us all, it is particularly so for young children. The incidence of skin cancer is rising at an alarming rate, and doctors believe that the sunburns that occur in young children often result in malignancies as these children age.

Doctors recommend that a sunscreen with an SPF of at least 15 be worn daily.

Although we cannot reverse the sun's damaging effects, we can do our best to prevent more.

Sunday May 24

Now unto the King eternal, immortal, invisible, the only wise God, be honour and glory, for ever and ever.

1 Timothy 1:17

Monday May 25

MEMORIAL DAY

This is Memorial Day, a holiday celebrated in the United States as a holiday to honour those who have passed before us.

Sleep, comrades, sleep and rest
On this Field of Grounded Arms,
Where foes no more molest,
Nor sentry's shot alarms!

Ye have slept on the ground before,
And started to your feet
At the cannon's sudden roar;
Or the drum's redoubling beat.

But in this Camp of Death
No sound your slumber breaks;
Here is no fevered breath,
No wound that bleeds and aches.

Rest comrades, rest and sleep!
The thoughts of men shall be
As sentinels to keep
Your rest from danger free.

Your silent tents of green
We deck with fragrant flowers;
Yours has the suffering been,
The memory shall be ours.

Henry Wadsworth Longfellow

Tuesday May 26

To know how to grow old is the master work of wisdom, and one of the most difficult chapters in the great art of living.

Wednesday May 27

We should so live and labour in our time that what came to us as seed may go to the next generation as blossom, and that which came to us as blossom may go to them as fruit.

Henry Ward Beecher

Thursday May 28

Tea baron Thomas Lipton was once on a steamer that ran aground. The captain ordered some of the cargo to be jettisoned in an effort to re-float his ship. As other passengers grabbed their belongings, Lipton spent his time stencilling "Drink Lipton's Tea" on everything that would float.

Friday May 29

Hotels become much busier as we get closer to summer. My daughter Julia related this story to me—I think you'll enjoy it too.

A gentleman arrived at a hotel in Montreal after a very long flight, only to be informed that his confirmed reservation could not be honoured because of an overbooking. There were no rooms.

"I will give you five minutes to find me a room," the man told the clerk, "and then I am going to undress in the lobby, put on my pyjamas and sleep on one of your sofas."

He got his room.

Saturday May 30

Try to keep things in perspective. Fifty years from now, kids in history class will be yawning over what panics us today.

Sunday May 31

A faithful friend is the medicine of life.

Ecclesiasticus 6:16, The Apocrypha

June

Monday June 1

This is the date of my wedding anniversary. It seems like but a brief time ago that I was a young bride walking down the aisle on my father's arm to join my handsome husband-to-be.

Although I wish our time together could have been longer, we enjoyed a full and happy life. It is with love and joy that I offer these words today:

Treasure the love you receive above all. It will survive long after your gold and good health have vanished.

Tuesday June 2

Success is best measured by how far you've come with the talents you've been given.

Wednesday June 3

I made a trip to the dentist today which I enjoyed very much. I find it difficult to believe that I actually said those words, because I used to live in dread of my twice-yearly visits. No matter what good care I gave my teeth, I never seemed able to escape without having one or more of them filled.

What progress there has been in this profession. Today I reclined in a comfortable chair while I listened to calming music through a set of earphones. The dental hygienist carefully cleaned my teeth and the dentist pronounced my teeth and gums healthy and without cavities. I felt as if I had enjoyed a half-hour social visit.

It wasn't always like this. Years ago the dentist's office was often attached to his home. Many dentists did their own lab work, and it was not uncommon for his wife to be cooking soup and sterilizing instruments in boiling water over the same kitchen stove.

Dentures needed to be vulcanized back then, and they too would have been "cooked" in his kitchen.

Instruments were crude and an anaesthetic was often a large shot of whisky or a small whiff of ether. Frequently work was done without benefit of either, and it was that experience that led me to dread the dentist.

Thank goodness for progress!

Thursday June 4

As I grow older more and more of my friends have passed away. It is very difficult to say goodbye to those whom we have loved, but I take comfort in the words of Helen Keller.

"With every friend I love who has been taken into the brown bosom of the earth a part of me has been buried there; but their contribution to my being of happiness, strength, and understanding remains to sustain me in an altered world."

Friday June 5

The true test of friendship is to be able to sit or walk with a friend for an hour in perfect silence without wearying of one another's company.

Dinah Maria Mulock Craik

Saturday June 6

Have faith and pursue the unknown end.

Oliver Wendell Holmes Jr.

Sunday June 7

'Mid all the traffic of the ways
Turmoils without, within—
Make in my heart a quiet place,
And come and dwell therein.

John Oxenham hymn

Monday June 8

I am writing this page today as I sit in the quiet woods near the millpond in our town. I have come to sit on this same stump for as long as I have lived with Marg and Bruce. This place provides some wonderful memories—catching butterflies with my grandchildren, evening walks with Marg and Bruce or a picnic with good friends.

My purpose in coming here alone today is to write, but it's also to clear my mind. The restorative properties of this setting are amazing. I can come here feeling tired or burdened and within a few hours I feel renewed, in body and soul.

I suppose that everyone has a place that they go when in need of "recharging the batteries." Any place where you can turn off the noise of the world will do. These are those necessary moments that strengthen and renew us.

Tuesday June 9

My goodness but time flies by. I can hardly believe that I am celebrating my birthday yet again.

Although I would be perfectly content to forget about it, the family seem unwilling to do so. (In fact it's quite nice to be fussed over and I always enjoy ice cream and cake.)

In keeping with a tradition started a few years ago, each person has taken the money that they would have spent on a gift for me and used it to do something special for themselves (or another) and then described it for me in a card or letter.

I was particularly pleased to hear that Jenny had purchased a pair of pearl stud earrings to be worn at her Grade 8 graduation ceremony.

"I'll be thinking of you, Gram, when I walk across the stage."

Several friends donated gifts (in my name) to the Cancer Society, while others chose to give to the Heart and Stroke Foundation.

I think my favourite gift of all was from my great-grandsons Mickey and Geoffrey, who delivered a beautiful rose to every resident of our local nursing home with a card attached that said, "With love from Edna."

It really was a special day.

Wednesday June 10

No steam or gas ever drives anything until it is confined. No Niagara is ever turned into light and power until it is tunneled. No life ever grows until it is focused, dedicated, disciplined.

Harry Emerson Fosdick

Thursday June 11

Probably the last completely accurate weather forecast was when God told Noah that there was a 100 percent chance of precipitation.

Friday June 12

What does he plant who plants a tree?
He plants the friend of sun and sky;
He plants the flag of breezes free;
The shaft of beauty towering high.

Henry C. Bunner

Saturday June 13

One of the things I enjoy most about the return to fine weather is the barbecued dinners that Bruce does so well. This evening's grilled sausage and potato salad was another of his culinary successes.

This recipe serves 6 people.
2 lb. small red potatoes, halved
5 tbsp. vegetable oil
1 bunch green onions
1 lb. turkey kielbasa
5 tbsp. cider vinegar
2 tbsp. sugar
1 tbsp. dijon prepared mustard
1 tbsp. water
1/4 tsp. salt, 1/4 tsp. ground black pepper

1. Heat barbecue grill. Coat grill rack with non-stick vegetable cooking spray. In large bowl toss potatoes with 1 tbsp. oil and grill over medium-hot coals, turning occasionally until well browned—about 20 minutes. Set bowl with remaining oil aside. Transfer potatoes to heavy aluminum foil, wrap, continue cooking over low heat until tender—about 20 minutes longer.
2. Trim roots off onions. Place in bowl used for potatoes and toss with oil remaining. Cut the kielbasa into 4 pieces.
3. Grill kielbasa and onions over medium-hot coals, turning frequently until browned—about 4 minutes. Remove onions and sausage to cutting board. Cut kielbasa into 1/4" thick slices, onion into 1" lengths and potato halves into 2 wedges.

4. In a jar combine 4 tbsp. oil, vinegar, sugar, mustard, water, salt and pepper until well mixed.
5. In a large serving bowl toss potatoes, onions and kielbasa with dressing. Serve immediately.

Sunday June 14

The Lord bless you and keep you. The Lord make his face to shine upon you, and be gracious unto you. The Lord lift up his countenance upon you, and give you peace, both now and evermore. Amen.

Book of Common Prayer

Monday June 15

As the school year comes to a close, Marg and Bruce have decided to celebrate by taking each of their grandchildren out to dinner to the restaurant of their choice.

This evening it was Bethany's turn and her selection proved to be rather a surprise. Marshall and Jamie thought that she would chose a fast-food outlet, but instead she choose a local Italian trattoria.

Dressed in her prettiest dress and "party" shoes, with ribbons in her hair, she joined Grandma and

Grampa for a wonderful meal served in an elegant ambience.

She kept her grandparents' rapt attention as she recalled highlights of the school year.

The evening was a huge success, and Marg and Bruce eagerly anticipate their time with the other grandchildren in their turn.

Tuesday June 16

A Greek sculptor once did a statue which he called "Opportunity." It stands on tiptoe to show how short a time it lingers; it has wings on its feet for it can fly quickly away; its front hair is long in order that men can seize it as it passes; the back of its head is bald because once past it can never be caught.

My thanks to one of my readers in the province of Alberta who passed the story on to me.

Wednesday June 17

Facts do not cease to exist because they are ignored.

Aldous Huxley

Thursday June 18

My interest is in the future—because I am going to spend the rest of my life there.

Charles F. Kettering

Friday June 19

Phyllis' husband Bill is an obstetrician in a large hospital. The nurses in that area of the hospital are kept pretty busy.

A nurse on duty was asked to check a young mother-to-be who arrived bright and early one morning.

"Is this your first baby?"

"Yes," replied the smiling young woman.

"Are you having pains and contractions?" asked the nurse.

"No," was the answer.

"Are you in some discomfort?" Again a negative reply.

"Well, why are you here?" the nurse asked.

"This is my due date," was her response.

The doctors and nurses have been laughing for weeks!

Saturday June 20

As one can ascend to the top of the house by means of a ladder or a bamboo or a staircase or a rope, so diverse are the ways and means to approach God, and every religion in the world shows one of these ways.

Ramakrishna

Sunday June 21

FATHER'S DAY

A dear friend of mine, Eoin MacIntyre, passed away in 1995. His daughter Robin wrote this short but poignant tribute to her father, and I would like to share it with you today.

For my father, life was an honourable gift, to be enjoyed and shared with joy.

He knew himself to be a part of the eternal mystery and energy that connects all living things, and he felt a responsibility to uphold and nurture that connection with love and care. There was no hierarchy in this kinship, all beings receiving the same kind attentions and interest.

Dad's belief in this energy of "being" extended beyond earthly things that he loved, and he often saved a poem or quote that echoed his thoughts, or delighted with its sentiment.

I'd like to share one of his favourites with you today.

The little cares that fretted me
I lost them yesterday,
Up in the hills above the sea,
Up where the poppies nod;
Where ill thoughts die and good are born
Up in the hills of God.

Truman Vancil

Monday June 22

Advice is like medicine—you have to take it to see if it does any good.

Tuesday June 23

Success is important, but so is the way we arrive there.

Bern Williams

Wednesday June 24

St. Jean Baptiste Day

This is St. Jean Baptiste Day in the province of Quebec. It is a day to celebrate their love of *La Belle Province* and to express pride in their heritage. Parades, speeches, picnics and many fireworks celebrations make it a wonderful day to be French Canadian.

Thursday June 25

Touched by a light that hath no name,
A glory never sung,
Aloft on sky and mountain wall
Are God's great pictures hung.

John Greenleaf Whittier

Friday June 26

Good words shall gain you honour in the market-place; but good deeds shall gain you friends among men.

Lao-tse

Saturday June 27

Nothing is more damaging to a new truth than an old error.

Goethe

Sunday June 28

O give thanks unto the Lord; for He is good: because his mercy endureth for ever.

Psalms 118:1

Monday June 29

I was unpacking a box of old china on the weekend when I came upon a Toby jug.

Originally created in Staffordshire, England, they appeared about 1760 and captured public fancy and popularity for generations.

For those of you not familiar with them, the Toby pitchers portray rotund figures with smiling faces. They stand about 9 1/2–10 inches tall and hold about one quart of liquid.

The "Ordinary Toby" depicts a portly seated gentleman with a beer mug in his hand. He wears a long coat, knee breeches and a tricorn hat whose corners form pouring spouts. The hats of all Tobys were originally made with small removable tops which may have served as cups, but very few of the tops have survived.

Old Tobys, particularly those made in the 18th century, are treasured by collectors for their beautiful colours and fine workmanship.

Royal Doulton continues to craft the jugs today and many of their works depict contemporary village characters or literary or historical figures.

Some of the jugs are extremely valuable, so if you have one of these treasures you may want to have it appraised. Mine may not be valuable but it holds many memories.

Tuesday June 30

Summer is here and I feel it in the heat of the sun at midday.

The fields abound with the beautiful Queen Anne's lace. A generous bunch of the flowers arranged in a vase brings summer into the kitchen.

The wind chime blowing in the breeze outside my window tinkles summer's arrival.

I welcome this beautiful season.

July

Wednesday July 1

CANADA DAY

Wilfrid Laurier, a former Canadian Prime Minister, said, "Let us show our children and all future generations that patriotism is only developed by the good citizens. Show our respect for the law, love of our Dominion's ideals and institutions and respect for our flag."

At a time when our country continues to grow and change, these are still wise words to live by.

Respect for all Canadians, no matter their country of origin, and pride in this beautiful country are ties that will bind us together from Atlantic to Pacific.

"O, Canada, Our Home!"

Thursday July 2

The youngsters in our neighbourhood seem to be very pleased to be on vacation. I hear their happy chatter early in the morning and later into the evening as they enjoy time free from the nightly ritual of homework.

Many of the children are taking advantage of the day-camps offered by our town. These camps run daily Monday to Friday and they offer a terrific alternative to an all-day babysitting situation.

Staffed by high school and university students, these camps offer a variety of activities from crafts to sports, daily swim time and bussed excursions to such venues as Ontario Place or Niagara Falls.

In homes where both parents are working, day-camps offer affordable care for the children and lots of fun and friendship for kids of all ages.

I almost wish that I were young again!

Friday July 3

Go oft to the house of thy friend, for weeds choke the unused path.

Ralph Waldo Emerson

Saturday July 4

For my many good friends in the United States, this day is "The Glorious Fourth." For these friends and all of our neighbours to the south I offer "Many Things to Me" by Jay Giammarino.

You are the blessed earth beneath my feet,
The quarried cliffs, the valleys wet with dew;
You are the endless fields of yellow wheat
And corn so tall it screens the land from view.
From soil made rich from rivers running wide
Your pointed pines reach up to touch the sky;
As land of bursting harvests you provide
The food for half the world in good supply.

A nation made of fifty states, all free
That stretch three thousand miles from east to
    west
United by a trying history
From Rockies down to Allegheny's breast.
You are America and stir my soul
With love for you and resolve to keep you whole.

Sunday July 5

B e of good cheer; I have overcome the world.

John 16:33

Monday July 6

W ithout question British Columbia is a province rich in magnificent scenery. From the exquisite coastline running from Prince Rupert to Vancouver, the Gulf Islands and Vancouver Island itself, inland to the Fraser Valley and on through the Rockies, B.C. offers a little of everything to the tourist.

My friends Martin and Rose McGillvery recently travelled through British Columbia, and their letters and postcards spoke with enthusiasm of all that they had seen.

One of the highlights of the trip for Rose was a ride on the Hell's Gate Airtram.

Located some 25 kilometres south of Boston Bar, the Airtram offers a ride over the Fraser River's narrowest gap, roughly 180 metres deep and 30 metres wide. The river surges through the gap at a rate of 7 metres per second.

The Airtram, suspended on a wire, gives a spectacular view of the raging water.

"For one who has difficulty standing on a chair the sensation was breathtaking. It took all my courage to get aboard but I wouldn't have missed it for the world!" wrote Rose.

Tuesday July 7

A rock pile ceases to be a rock pile the moment a single man contemplates it, bearing within him the image of a cathedral.

Antoine de Saint-Exupéry

Wednesday July 8

Tomorrow our family will celebrate the birthday of my great-grandchildren Jenny and Justin. As I look on these two youngsters who will become teenagers tomorrow, I can't help but remember the day in 1985 when they were born.

As is often the case, the twins came early and were quite tiny.

I remember that I laughed as Justin, wee little thing that he was, screwed up his tiny face like a raisin and let out one almighty yell, greatly startling the nurse who was caring for him in the nursery.

Jenny lay there, as sweet and as quiet as could be, eyes open, seeming to take in her new world with a quiet calm nature that stays with her today.

It is hard to imagine that these beautiful young people were ever so small.

I guess my age is showing.

Thursday July 9

Mohandas K. Gandhi, who successfully led India's drive for independence, often changed his mind publicly. An aide once asked him how he could so often contradict this week what he had said just last week. The great man replied, "That is because this week I know better."

Friday July 10

Sometimes the best helping hand you can get is a good, firm push.

Saturday July 11

My grandson Fred is building a new deck on his house, and he spent several hours at the local lumberyard.

The customer ahead of him in line was obviously new at this business.

"Where do you keep your two by fours?" he inquired.

"How long do you want them?" asked the salesman pointing to the pile.

"Quite a while, actually. I'm nailing them to my house."

Sunday July 12

Let us run with patience the race that is set before us,

Looking unto Jesus the author and finisher of our faith.

Hebrews 12:1–2

Monday July 13

The chance of things going wrong with a golf shot goes up in direct proportion to the number of people watching.

M. Huston

My grandson Marshall can attest to the verity of those words. This past Saturday he was involved in a celebrity tournament to raise funds for juvenile diabetes research. Each participant was paired up with a well-known personality, and it was Marshall's luck to draw a star-status hockey player (who is also an outstanding golfer).

As Marshall stepped up to the tee his nerves got the better of him. He teed up the ball, took a mighty swing and watched, horrified, as his ball moved about a foot and half onto the fairway.

"Oh boy," murmured his partner, "could be a long day."

The crowd politely said nothing.

Tuesday July 14

A child enters your home and for the next twenty years makes so much noise that you can hardly stand it. Then the child departs, leaving the house so silent that you think you are going mad.

John Andrew Holmes

Wednesday July 15

A lie has no legs. It requires other lies to support it. Tell one lie and you are forced to tell other lies to back it up.

Thursday July 16

The supreme happiness of life is the conviction of being loved for yourself, or more correctly, being loved in spite of yourself.

Victor Hugo

Friday July 17

My good friend Mary McConnell is the mother of ten children. Vacations for her and her husband were few and far between. One year, however, as an anniversary gift the two of them enjoyed a holiday in Nassau, in the Bahamas.

"It was heavenly, Edna. We got up when we felt like it, read books endlessly as we sat by the pool and enjoyed romantic candlelight dinners in the evening. One thing can bring memories of that trip back like no other—the smell of a Piña Colada.

"Often in the summer if I know that the children will be away during the day I will have a Piña Colada Smoothie, close my eyes and reminisce about that wonderful trip."

You don't need to have been there to enjoy this delicious breakfast treat.

1/2 cup chilled evaporated skim milk
1/2 tsp. coconut extract
1/4 ripe banana, peeled and frozen
1/4 cup pineapple chunks, frozen
2 or 3 ice cubes

In a blender combine the milk and the coconut extract. Add frozen banana and a few pineapple pieces; blend. Add the rest of the fruit pieces and the ice cubes and blend until smooth.

Saturday July 18

This is a household hint for those of you who enjoy camping or have children who will be going off to overnight camp this summer.

Store your sleeping bags with a fabric softener sheet inside. This will keep them smelling as fresh as just-washed.

Sunday July 19

This is one of my favourite hymns. I sang it at church this morning and it filled me with an inner peace as few other hymns can do.

Abide with me, fast falls the eventide
The darkness deepens, Lord with me abide;
When other helpers fail, and comforts flee,
Help of the helpless, Lord abide with me.

Hold Thou Thy Cross before my closing eyes;
Shine through the gloom and point me to the
   skies
Heaven's morning breaks and earth's vain shad-
   ows flee;
In life, in death, O Lord, abide with me.

Monday July 20

Alysia Gabriel died two years ago today, on her 17th birthday, but the impact that she made in her short life will be felt for years to come.

Lou, as her friends called her, died of cystic fibrosis, that horrible disease that attacks children and young adults. But she didn't go without a fight or without doing everything that she could to help find a cure.

When she was diagnosed with CF at 5 months, her parents, who knew little about the disease, decided that they would fight it with her and help her win.

Alysia put her efforts into fund-raising at a very early age. At age 5 she appeared on a CF poster and she took part regularly in radiothons and community events to raise funds for research. She even threw out the first pitch at the Blue Jays game on her 16th birthday.

In all the projects she did along the way, she felt she was achieving something and helping other CF sufferers. She hoped and wished for a cure. She was making a difference.

When her father died of a heart attack in 1991 she and her brother Barrett became even closer to each other and to mom Michelle.

Mostly, though, she was just "Lou," friend to many, member of the Milton District High School cheerleading squad, girlfriend of Gareth Llewellan and a "regular" teenager.

Oh, but how much more she was!

Tuesday July 21

Flowers always make people better, happier, and more helpful; they are sunshine, food and medicine to the soul.

Luther Burbank

Wednesday July 22

As I sat in the garden today I was reminded of this poem, "To a Butterfly" by William Wordsworth.

I've watched you now a full half-hour,
Self-poised upon that yellow flower;
And little Butterfly! indeed
I know not if you sleep or feed.
How motionless!—not frozen seas
More motionless! and then
What joy awaits you, when the breeze
Hath found you out among the trees,
And calls you forth again!

This plot of orchard-ground is ours;
My trees they are, my Sister's flowers;
Here rest your wings when they are weary;
Here lodge as in a sanctuary!
Come often to us, fear no wrong;
Sit near us on the bough!
We'll talk of sunshine and of song,
And summer days, when we were young;
Sweet childish days, that were as long
As twenty days are now.

Thursday July 23

Today is Marg and Bruce's wedding anniversary. Their plan is to have a few friends over for dinner and to enjoy a quiet evening at home. What they don't know is that their children have made other arrangements.

At 6 p.m., when they think that guests are arriving, a limousine will appear at the door to pick them up. The limo will drive them to Niagara-on-the-Lake, where they have a lovely suite waiting at the Prince of Wales Hotel and dinner reservations in the dining room for eight o'clock.

Tomorrow morning they will enjoy brunch and an afternoon performance at the Shaw Festival, after which the limousine will bring them home.

The children have had such fun arranging this surprise for their parents. They have planned every detail with love and care, and they are hardly able to contain their excitement.

You know that parents have done something right when their children have turned out so well.

Friday July 24

There is no pillow so soft as a clear conscience.

Saturday July 25

I watched our neighbour Norm as he worked to teach his young daughter how to ride her bicycle today. His method was so clever that I thought I would pass it on.

He took a large towel, folded lengthwise, and wrapped it around Robin's tummy. He held on to the ends in one hand.

As Robin started to pedal, Norm pulled tightly on the towel to keep Robin upright and balanced on the bicycle. When it seemed that she was steady he would loosen his grip just a little and she would be balancing on her own. When she wobbled, Norm would pull up on the towel and she would regain her balance.

In a very short time Robin had a feel for the balance and soon she was riding on her own with confidence.

This method seems to save on bumps, bruises and tears that usually go with this learning venture.

Sunday July 26

The Lord is nigh unto all them that call upon him.

Psalms 145:18

Monday July 27

In the area where Sarah and Richard live the roads are laid out in a rather haphazard way. It is not unusual for people unfamiliar with the area to become lost.

One day last week, a bewildered-looking driver stopped and asked Richard if he could direct him to the Hutchisons' home. Richard gave him directions, then mentioned, "You know Brian

Hutchison was transferred. The family doesn't live there any more."

"I know," the driver answered sheepishly. "I do."

Tuesday July 28

It is not how much we have, but how much we enjoy, that makes happiness.

Robertson Davies

Wednesday July 29

Nothing prevents us from being natural so much as the desire to appear so.

Duc de La Rochefoucauld

Thursday July 30

Lila and I enjoyed the afternoon together, reading and drinking iced tea in the garden. I missed her company very much while she was in hospital and I am so happy that she is home and feeling well again.

"You know, Edna, for a time I thought that I might not get well again or be able to come home. It's pretty frightening when you are alone in a hospital room and feeling dreadful. Then gradually

I began to think about all the things that I have enjoyed in this life and soon I began to see that even if I were to die I have had a wonderful life. Somehow when I realized this it was as if I could relax and be at peace with whatever was to come along. It was then that I began to get well and now…well, here I am."

I treasure her friendship and I'm happy to have her home.

Friday July 31

Chance makes brothers—hearts make friends.

Dr. Duane Booth

August

Saturday August 1

No matter how much we enjoy a holiday, there is something special about coming home. These few lines came back to me as I savoured my morning tea.

So I set off when gypsy blood
Wells up and urges me to start,
I wander on and on until
Homesickness strikes my heart.

World travel has its golden days
And it is nice at times to roam,
But far the best part of adventure:
Return to Home Sweet Home.

Sunday August 2

Thou shalt love the Lord thy God with all thy heart, and with all thy soul, and with all thy strength, and with all thy mind.

Luke 10:27

Monday August 3

This is the Civic Holiday and our family took advantage of the day by enjoying a picnic.

We lunched today at the Ball's Falls Conservation Area and Historic Park near the town of Jordan.

This area was settled in the late 18th century by Loyalists crossing the United States border. These settlements were named according to their location in miles from the border. The area in which Jordan was founded was known as The Twenty.

There is much to see here: the Jordan Historical Museum, a Mennonite churchyard, a rare 19th-century fruit press, and a stone schoolhouse.

Ball's Falls, nearby, provides a perfect woodland setting for a picnic. This area is easily reached and is a terrific place to spend a warm summer's day.

Tuesday August 4

I remain to this day an admirer of the British Royal family and I always enjoy stories about its members.

Queen Mary, wife of King George V, was an avid collector of antiques. This could sometimes pose a problem, however, for when she visited the private home of one of her subjects any prized antique that was admired by the Queen, according to etiquette, had to be presented to her.

On one occasion, though, Queen Mary, visiting an exhibition of antiques, noticed that one piece was missing from a collection of Wedgwood china. "I believe I have seen that piece somewhere in Buckingham Palace," she remarked.

That evening a car drew up at the exhibition and out stepped Queen Mary, the missing piece in hand. She had taken the trouble to find the piece and deliver it personally to an astonished exhibitor.

Wednesday August 5

B e able to be alone. Lose not the advantage of solitude.

Sir Thomas Browne

Thursday August 6

People who clamor to be "free" (which usually means rid of their obligations) forget Goethe's warning: "Everything that frees our spirit without giving us control of ourselves is ruinous."

Sydney J. Harris

Friday August 7

Between our birth and death we may touch understanding as a moth brushes a window with its wing.

Christopher Fry

Saturday August 8

When asked if he ever looked up to the galleries of the House of Lords to see if there was anybody listening to him, Lord Ramsey, the former Archbishop of Canterbury, replied with a smile, "I am always looking upward to see if there's anybody there."

Sunday August 9

Glory to Thee who safe has kept
And hath refreshed me whilst I slept
Grant, Lord, when I from death shall wake,
I may of endless light partake.

Bishop Thomas Ken

Monday August 10

Today finds me in Muskoka again for my annual visit with Eleanor. How I delight in being in this beautiful area! Today was especially enjoyable as Eleanor had invited mutual friends to join us for a boat cruise up through the locks at Port Carling and into Lake Joseph.

We made our way very slowly so as to fully appreciate the beauty of the rocks, the trees and the water en route. It brought to my mind this Indian song:

High on a rocky ledge
I build my wigwam
Close to the water's edge
Silent and still
Blue lake and rocky shore
I will return once more
Boom di di ah di boom.

Tuesday August 11

This morning something strange occurred that took me back forty years to a memory that I had nearly forgotten.

As I lay in bed reading I turned on the radio, hoping to hear the news and weather. As I fiddled with the dial I suddenly heard the announcer say "And this is WOWO, Fort Wayne, Indiana." For whatever reason, on a warm summer's evening such as this, the radio waves seem to take strange turns and we are able to pick up stations that are hundreds and hundreds of miles away.

On just such a night as this in 1958, George and the girls and I were staying at a cottage near Parry Sound, Ontario. The girls were in bed when George turned on the radio and what should we hear but "This is WOWO, Fort Wayne, Indiana, presenting an evening of the best of jazz!"

George, a jazz music fan, was ecstatic. Soon the two of us were dancing to music from such greats as Benny Goodman, Tommy and Jimmy Dorsey, Lionel Hampton and others. We danced well into the night, enjoying the magic of the radio orchestras from so far away.

I'll be dancing in my dreams again tonight.

Wednesday August 12

To own a bit of ground, to scratch it with a hoe, to plant seeds, and watch the renewal of life— this is the commonest delight of the race, the most satisfactory thing a man can do.

Charles Dudley Warner

Thursday August 13

Give us grace and strength to forbear and to persevere. Give us courage and gaiety and the quiet mind, spare to us our friends, soften to us our enemies.

Robert Louis Stevenson

Friday August 14

To renew ties with the past need not always be daydreaming; it may be tapping old sources of strength for new tasks.

Simeon Strunsky

Saturday August 15

A "not to be missed" event here in Muskoka, and probably in most cottage areas through-out the country, is the Aquatic Regatta.

In Muskoka each individual cottage association organizes and runs the events for the cottagers in their area.

It was a beautiful sunny day today and the weather provided a superb backdrop for the regatta held in the bay very near Eleanor's cottage.

As usual the day afforded a great opportunity for the young and the young-at-heart to compete or to share vicariously the competition in many and varied aquatic events.

There were the usual swimming races for various age groups, canoe races for individual paddlers or groups of two or four, during competitions and sailing races.

What I enjoyed most, however, were the "fun" races. The "hand paddle canoe race" saw 10 people in each canoe leaning over the side and, using only their hands as paddles, trying to race to shore. It took great skill to remain in the canoe, and several of the canoes tipped. Watching 10 people trying to get back into the righted canoe had Eleanor and me holding our sides, we were laughing so hard.

A barbecue dinner was enjoyed by all and seemed to be the perfect end to a fun-filled day.

Sunday August 16

Forsake not an old friend, for the new is not comparable to him. A new friend is as new wine; when it is old thou shalt drink it with pleasure.

Ecclesiasticus 9:10, The Apocrypha

Monday August 17

Evenings at the cottage are sometimes the loveliest part of the day. Dinner has been eaten, the dishes are washed, dried and put away and it is a few hours until bed time. What shall we do?

Eleanor and I had a quick answer for that question—Scrabble.

We played at a table set up on the porch and it was a very close game, each of us scoring reasonably well while restricting ourselves to just a few strange spellings of even stranger words.

Actually Eleanor is quite good at that part of the game. She will lay her letters on the board with just the right amount of confidence as if to say "Don't challenge this one, Edna—I know it's a real word!" She can even come up with what seem to be appropriate meanings—again with just enough authority in her voice to counter any objection on my part.

Ah yes, to play Scrabble with Eleanor is to play with a master.

Tuesday August 18

All I have seen teaches me to trust the Creator for all I have not seen.

Ralph Waldo Emerson

Wednesday August 19

Henry David Thoreau wrote of an evening spent at Walden Pond:

I sit in my boat on Walden, playing the flute this evening, and see the perch, which I seem to have charmed, hovering around me, and the moon travelling over the bottom, which is strewn with the wrecks of the forest, and feel that nothing but the wildest imagination can conceive of the manner of life we are living. Nature is a wizard. The Concord nights are stranger than the Arabian nights.

Thursday August 20

The nearest way to glory is to strive to be what you wish to be thought to be.

Socrates

Friday August 21

People are lonely because they build walls instead of bridges.

Saturday August 22

I shall be leaving Muskoka tomorrow but I shall be taking many wonderful memories with me. My friendship with Eleanor goes back decades and so our time together has the feel of an old slipper—worn but truly comfortable. These friendships are rare and because this is so they are to be cherished.

It is great to have friends when one is young, but indeed it is still more so when one is getting old. When one is young, friends are, like everything else, a matter of course. In the older years one knows what it means to have them.

Edvard Grieg

Sunday August 23

Look upon the rainbow and praise him that made it.

Ecclesiasticus 38:25, The Apocrypha

Monday August 24

While driving home yesterday Marg and I stopped at a fast-food restaurant on the highway. Despite incredible popularity, this type of eatery is not a 20th-century phenomenon. Ancient Romans, for example, would stop for a bowl of stew or a plate of vegetables at street stalls in the marketplace.

However, if we are looking for the beginnings of our present-day fast foods, it could well be back in 1902. Frank Hardart and his partner Joe Horn opened a new type of restaurant in which the customers served their own food. The foods were displayed in compartments behind glass windows. To get the food they wanted, customers had only to drop the right change into the slot. These restaurants were known as "automats."

In the late 1920s Howard Deering Johnson was selling home-made ice cream in his patent medicine store in Wollaston, Massachusetts. Later he would sell his ice cream at Massachusetts beaches, an idea that he soon expanded to include roadside restaurants. Howard Johnson's "28 flavours of ice cream" were soon appreciated coast-to-coast.

In 1954 Ray Kroc saw a drive-in restaurant, in San Bernardino, California, crowded with customers buying hamburgers and milkshakes. He convinced Richard and Maurice McDonald, the owners, to let him franchise the restaurant. The rest is "over 50 billion served" history now.

Tuesday August 25

The turning points of lives are not the great moments. The real crises are often concealed in occurrences so trivial in appearance that they pass unobserved.

William E. Woodward

Wednesday August 26

The chill in the evening air is a reminder that the summer is coming to a close. So too are the red and yellow leaves that are beginning to be seen in the woods, another notice that autumn is just around the corner.

Although I look forward to the beauty of the fall season I shall miss the long warm days of summer. Evening walks by the pond are enjoyed at an earlier hour now and often with a sweater on the shoulders to ward off the crispness of the air.

I love autumn but, oh, how I shall miss summer.

Autumn creeps in on moccasins silent as the Harvest Moon.

H. Borland

Thursday August 27

A visit to our local mall today gave further proof that summer is nearing its close. Mothers and their children were engaged in that popular "end of summer-school is beginning" activity—buying school clothes and school supplies.

This is always an interesting ritual. The children choose, mother looks aghast; mother chooses, children look stricken and threaten to boycott school for the year.

'Twas ever thus....I remember shopping with the girls when they were young and clothing selections became a contest of wills. "Young lady, you may *not* wear that outfit to school!" was my mantra. "But that's what *everybody* is wearing!" was the reply.

Somehow we managed to come to an amicable agreement about what to buy, and apparently so did their friends and their mothers, because inevitably on the first day of school all of the youngsters were dressed in nearly identical attire.

The more things change the more they stay the same....

Friday August 28

There is nothing like sealing a letter to inspire a fresh thought.

Saturday August 29

The young do not know enough to be prudent, and therefore they attempt the impossible—and achieve it, generation after generation.

Pearl S. Buck

Sunday August 30

The Lord is at hand. Be careful for nothing; but in every thing by prayer and supplication with thanksgiving let your requests be made known unto God.

Philippians 4:5–6

Monday August 31

Kind words can be short and easy to speak, but their echoes are truly endless.

Mother Teresa

September

Tuesday September 1

Fading light
Dims the sight,
And a star gems the sky,
Gleaming bright,
From afar,
Drawing nigh,
Falls the night.

Dear one, rest!
In the west
Sable night
Lulls the day on her breast.
Sweet, goodnight!
Now away
To thy rest.

Love, sweet dreams!
Lo, the beams
Of the light
Fairy moon kiss the streams.
Love, good night!
Ah, so soon!
Peaceful dreams!

These words of "Taps" came to mind as I enjoyed the beautiful first sunset of September.

Wednesday September 2

Although education has displayed many changes over the years, the expectations of parents have not. Then and now parents have wanted the best possible education for their children.

In Funk and Wagnall's *The Literary Digest* of July 1, 1916, I came across an advertisement for Bordertown Military Institute in Bordertown, New Jersey. It reads:

Purpose: The individual development of a boy's character and scholarship for the work of the world in college, scientific school or business.

Faculty: A large, sympathetic and efficient body of instructors. 31 years of experience.

Instruction: Small classes, individual attention. Each boy is taught *how* to study.

Location: Healthful location on the Delaware River seven miles from Trenton on the Pennsylvania River.

School Life: High standards of social and moral student life. Supervised athletics, wholesome food, carefully regulated daily program of work and recreation and drill produce sound bodies, capable minds and cheerful dispositions.

What parent could ask for more? Although written more than 90 years ago it could serve as an excellent standard for today's students.

Thursday September 3

E very day one should at least hear one little song, read one good poem, see one fine painting and—if at all possible—speak a few sensible words.

Goethe

Friday September 4

Wishing you
    A house full of sunshine,
    Hearts full of cheer,
    Love that grows deeper
    Each day of the year.

From an old Welsh blessing

Saturday September 5

I beg you, do not be unchangeable. Do not believe that you alone can be right. The man who thinks that, the man who maintains that only he has the power to reason correctly, the gift to speak the soul—a man like that, when you know him, turns out empty.

Sunday September 6

Lighten our darkness we beseech thee, O Lord; and by thy great mercy defend us from all perils and dangers of this night.

An evening prayer

Monday September 7

LABOUR DAY

The Labour Day holiday marks the last long weekend of summer. In some areas there are parades to celebrate this day; in others it is merely a day off to enjoy before the start of school tomorrow.

Abraham Lincoln, in a message to Congress, had this to say about labour.

Inasmuch as most good things are produced by labour, it follows that all such things ought to belong to those whose labour has produced them. But it has happened in all ages of the world that some have laboured, and others, without, have enjoyed a larger proportion of the fruits. This is wrong, and should not continue. To secure to each labourer the whole product of his labour as nearly as possible is a worthy object of any good government.

Tuesday September 8

In most areas of our province, today marks the return to school for both elementary and secondary school students.

For my great-grandchildren Justin and Jenny it is the first day of high school. Both of them are extremely excited about this—not so much because of the academics but rather because of the sports programs. Justin has high hopes of making the football team, while Jenny has her heart set on being a member of the cheerleading squad. Both youngsters have worked hard all summer to get in shape for the tryouts. Running, aerobics and weight-training were part of a daily fitness regimen that they hope will earn them a spot on their chosen team. If hard work counts for anything they should be successful in their endeavours.

"Oh, and as well, they may be able to find time to fit in a few classes," remarked Phyllis dryly.

Wednesday September 9

When someone tells you that something defies description you can be pretty sure he's going to have a go at it anyway.

Thursday September 10

At this time of year tomatoes are at their delicious best. With the help of my friend Will we have planted a number of tomato plants that have proven to be prolific. We have hundreds of tomatoes of many different varieties. Thankfully I have an enormous number of recipes that will use a great many of them in a variety of ways.

On occasion we pick some of the tomatoes before they are ripe. (I absolutely love fried green tomato sandwiches.)

If you have been given tomatoes that are not quite ripe I have a few hints from Will to help you ripen them to perfection.

1. Store your tomatoes at room temperature, preferably in a bowl with other fruit. This will speed ripening. Refrigeration prevents ripening and kills the flavour.
2. Do not ripen tomatoes on a window sill, as the sun softens them but does not help them ripen.
3. Don't store tomatoes stem side down, as the rounded "shoulders" will bruise from the weight of the fruit.
4. You may freeze ripe tomatoes to be used later in soups and stews. Rinse them and gently pat them dry. Freeze them, whole, in a plastic freezer bag.

Friday September 11

A kind word is never lost. It keeps going on and on, from one person to another, until at last it comes back to you again.

Saturday September 12

Here in Canada there was a very common expression "Keeping up with the Joneses." Jones was, and still is, a very common name, and that expression of course meant that you tried to keep pace with your neighbours in the possessions that you acquired.

In Seoul, South Korea, you would have to keep with the Kims. 21.9 percent of the population in this large city has the family name Kim, followed by Lee with 14.9 percent and Park with 8.5 percent.

South Korea has only 249 family names in use.

Imagine trying to look up a phone number in a South Korean phone book!

Sunday September 13

It is good that a man should both hope and quietly wait for the salvation of the Lord.

Lamentations 3:26

Monday September 14

Marshall and Jamie work with the youngsters in the Sunday school at the church.

"You know, Gran, even though we use the newer version of the Bible there are still some words and concepts that the children have trouble understanding. Here are a few that I thought you might get a kick out of."

Adultery is the sin of saying that you're older than you really are.

Joan of Arc was Noah's wife.

Our father who art in Heaven,
Harold be thy name.

Fast days are days when you have to eat in a hurry.

An epistle is the wife of an apostle.

Parsimony is what the parson lives on.

Round John Virgin is one of the twelve opossums.

Tuesday September 15

Need something done? Give the job to a busy person.

Wednesday September 16

I have enrolled in a night school class for this term. For some time I have wanted to be more proficient on the computer. Many people probably wonder why someone of my age would want to increase their computer skill level. I suppose that it does seem rather strange but I have always felt that while I am alive I should be learning something new as often as possible. My family, both young and old, have encouraged me to use the computer and I am able to handle very basic skills. Now it is time for me to learn more advanced uses. I certainly hope that our instructor is able to teach a "very old dog" a new trick.

Thursday September 17

While filling out an application form our neighbour wondered, "Is there any reason they would need to know my exact weight?"

"Of course not," her husband answered. "Just fill in 'over.'"

Friday September 18

Living on a fixed income, as many of us seniors are, is not always easy. Things that we took for granted such as travelling or meals in restaurants or entertainment at theatres have now become prohibitively expensive in many cases.

A good friend of mine seems to have dealt with her problem in a rather novel but practical way. Widowed several years ago, Mildred was left with a large house and taxes to match. Reluctant to give up the home that she knew and loved, she spent many an hour trying to come up with a workable plan.

Finally she called three good friends, also widows, whom she knew were living in apartments and not very pleased about it. Shortly thereafter, the three friends had happily moved in with Mildred and, by cost-sharing, had made their lives less lonely and less expensive.

This may not be a perfect solution for everyone but it certainly is working well for Mildred and her friends.

They all laugh when their friends call them "The Golden Girls."

Saturday September 19

The smallest act of kindness is worth more than the grandest intention.

Sunday September 20

How excellent is thy lovingkindness, O God! therefore the children of men put their trust under the shadow of thy wings.

Psalms 36:7

Monday September 21

The seasons change so quickly. Autumn has arrived and it is the season of abundance. Flowers, fruits and vegetables are being harvested and the countryside is a veritable horn of plenty.

The leaves are changing quickly now and they are beautiful almost beyond our ability to appreciate them.

Who could have thought of autumn?
An Artist's power has wrought
And spread to view a picture
Beyond mere human thought.

E.M. Shields

Tuesday September 22

Sometimes a neighbour whom we have disliked for a lifetime for his arrogance and conceit lets fall a single commonplace remark that shows us another side, another man really; a man uncertain, and puzzled, and in the dark like ourselves.

Willa Sibert Cather

Wednesday September 23

I bought a pepper squash at the market today. Squash is one of my favourite vegetables but I know that it isn't usually a popular vegetable among the younger set.

I vividly remember Margaret serving squash to Phyllis and Marshall and it received a very chilly reception. Margaret persevered, however (not wisely as things turned out), and insisted that the children "Try just a small mouthful."

Phyllis took a bite and quickly washed it down with milk. Marshall took a bite, gagged, swallowed and then threw up his entire dinner.

Margaret never insisted on their "trying it" again.

Thursday September 24

An alarm clock is a mechanism to scare the daylights into you.

Friday September 25

In autumn, breezes cool,
Mark the end of summer's rule…
Fragrant mow and laden bin.
Prove the harvest's gathered in.

Shorter day and longer night,
Winging birds in homeward flight
Haze of blue the woods enfold,
Falling maples red and gold.

In autumn, colour flares
From the bounty nature spares…
Richer, brighter still it glows
Than midsummer ever shows.

And the crickets mournfully
Sing of winter soon to be…
Light the lamp and close the door,
Summer's gone its way once more.

My thanks to the author, whose name is not known
to me.

Saturday September 26

Don't forget, even when you can't see it the
sun is shining behind the clouds.

Sunday September 27

This Sunday's service was the service of baptism. What a marvellous sight it was to see the seven beautiful children as they were received into Christ's flock. Two of the babies were wearing christening gowns that had clearly been handed down for several generations.

And they brought young children to him, that he should touch them: and his disciples rebuked those that brought them. But when Jesus saw it, he was much displeased, and said unto them, Suffer the little children to come unto me, and forbid them not: for of such is the kingdom of God.

Mark 10:13–14

Monday September 28

A college student wrote home to her mother, "Please send me some stamps. They are so expensive here."

Tuesday September 29

Prayer change things? No! Prayer changes people, and people change things.

Burton Hillis

Wednesday September 30

Resolve to be tender with the young, compassionate with the aged, sympathetic with the striving, and tolerant with the weak and the wrong. Sometime in life you will have been all of these.

October

Thursday October 1

What are the things I love to see
In autumn when the year grows old?
The black gum leaves of scarlet red;
A hillside poplar turned to gold.

What are the things I love to hear
In autumn when the year is spent?
The wild geese flying overhead,
And drowsy rain with its clean scent.

What are the things I love to smell
In autumn when the year is done?
Blue curling smoke from burning leaves
And wild grapes purpling in the sun.

Ah, autumn in her passing leaves
The memory of a lovely song
And for the heart a legacy
That will last all the winter long.

October has arrived in all its glory. Enjoy the
beauty now, for its memories will need to last
through the long cold winter.

Friday October 2

A friend is what the heart needs all the time.

Henry van Dyke

Saturday October 3

The Fall Fair has become an annual outing for us, and this year was no exception. What is so nice about these fairs is that there is something for everyone to enjoy.

This year we had a personal interest in the fair, as Marg had entered her home-made chili in the food fair contest and Phyllis and a group of her friends had done a lovely quilt to be judged at a quilting exhibit.

Marg's chili won a shiny blue first-place ribbon as well as the "Best of Competition" red, white and blue award. Bethany was thrilled by this and told everyone around here for the next several hours, "Grammie's chili won, Grammie's chili won."

Phyllis' quilting group also received a "Judges' Choice" award for their Sunflower Burst quilt.

As usual, though, the McCann "Best of Fair" award went to the hardworking ladies of the church who provided us with a turkey dinner fit for a king!

The fair was a huge success as usual.

Sunday October 4

The Lord is my strength and my shield; my heart trusted in Him, and I am helped: therefore my heart greatly rejoiceth; and with my song will I praise Him.

Psalms 28:7

Monday October 5

Each friend represents a world in us, a world possibly not born until they arrive, and it is only by this meeting that a new world is born.

Anaïs Nin

Tuesday October 6

This won't come as any surprise to the parents of teenagers, but Canada is one of the three most talkative nations in the world. We have more than 20,000,000 telephones in this country. If Alexander Graham Bell had earned a nickel for each phone call made last year, he would have been a billionaire.

I can think of very few inventions that have made more impact than the telephone—oh, excuse me, my phone is ringing.

Wednesday October 7

One of the members of my seniors' group hosted a luncheon today at her home. It was a gourmet delight, but what made it more special was that we were each given a lovely remembrance.

Marjory had made a beautiful herb wreath that was hung inside her front door.

She used 3 or 4 dried sprigs of different herbs—rosemary, sage, thyme and bay leaves—which she held together with a small elastic band. Then each was tied with a bow of 1/2" wide ribbon, either green or burgundy in colour.

Using florist's pins, Marjory attached the herbs to a 10" round straw wreath, and the effect was quite lovely. Each of us was given a herb bunch as we left.

I have pinned my bunch to a small pincushion on my dresser. It will remind me of a most enjoyable day and a very thoughtful hostess.

Thursday October 8

Success covers a multitude of blunders.

George Bernard Shaw

Friday October 9

What a fine afternoon this was, and the good weather gave me the chance to see Justin and Jenny at the high school football field.

Justin is a member of the football team, and this afternoon he was playing an important playoff game. Justin, being a grade 9 and therefore less experienced, spent much of his time cheering from the sidelines. However, as the score mounted in our favour, the coach began substituting his younger players. I was a very proud great-grandmother, cheering each time Justin handled the ball.

It was also a great thrill for me to see Jenny with her cheerleading team, leading the crowd with incredible enthusiasm.

The cheerleaders are members of a "power squad"—that is to say, they climb pyramids and do throws and catches that have me pretty much holding my breath with every cheer.

It's easy to see that these girls have put in many long hours in the practice gym in order to do these stunts safely.

It was a splendid afternoon for all of the athletes, and girls and boys alike were able to enjoy the thrill of victory.

Saturday October 10

This is the Thanksgiving weekend and, as is our family custom, many of us will come together to give thanks for all that we enjoy. We will be a large group this year, as both my sister and my brother and their families will join us.

Thankfully my grandson Fred and his wife June have a home in the country with a very large dining room. I think with a little luck (and a lot of planning) we may all just be able to squeeze in.

The nicest part about a family Thanksgiving is that everyone chips in to help so that the burden of the dinner preparation doesn't fall upon one person.

Family truly is a blessing that I am thankful for every day, but even more so as we join together to enjoy this happy holiday.

Sunday October 11

This is the blessing that we enjoy using before our Thanksgiving dinner.

Bless, O Lord, this food to our use, and consecrate us to thy service, and make us ever mindful of the needs of others; through Jesus Christ our Lord. Amen.

Monday October 12

THANKSGIVING DAY

It was wonderful to have a great number of our family together. It has been a long time since so many of us have enjoyed a family gathering. There were all of the usual comments—"My, how you've grown," "You look wonderful," "Your new hairstyle is beautiful"—before we could settle in to really catch up on the happenings of both young and old.

It was very interesting for me to see how strong our family resemblance is from one generation to the next. My brother Ben has a great-grand-child who looks just like Ben did at the same age.

Phyllis looks very much like Marg, and Marg looks more like my husband George every day.

I guess this is one of nature's wonders. Each of us is an individual and yet we carry something from every person who is a part of our heritage. I find it comforting to think that some small part of me will still be here enjoying Thanksgiving many generations from now.

For this Thanksgiving Day, O Lord,
To you our thanks we give.

Tuesday October 13

Leftover turkey usually highlights the dinner tables across our country this week. Marg has an easy but delicious recipe for Turkey Stuffing Bake to share with you that will provide at least one use for the bird scraps.

1 package commercial herbed seasoned stuffing
1 cup whole cranberry sauce
1/2 cup chopped walnuts or pecans
2 cups chopped turkey
1 1/2 cups turkey gravy (either leftover or
    canned)

Prepare the stuffing according to package directions.

In a medium bowl, combine prepared stuffing, cranberry sauce and nuts; set aside.

In a 2-quart oblong baking dish, arrange turkey evenly on the bottom. Pour gravy over the turkey. Spoon the stuffing mixture evenly over the turkey.

Bake in a pre-heated 400°F oven for 15 minutes or until hot and bubbling.

Serves 4.

Wednesday October 14

John Kenneth Galbraith shared with an audience his wife's comments on the length of his speeches:

"People may not be a great deal wiser after my talks, she says, but they are always a great deal older."

Thursday October 15

All good books are alike in that they are truer than if they really happened and after you are finished reading one you will feel it all happened to you, and afterwards it all belongs to you.

Ernest Hemingway

Friday October 16

I pity parents who cling to their children and try to live their lives instead of enjoying things that are open to themselves alone. Lay away a tool and it gets rusty. Lay away your own hobbies, friends, activities, and you will kill your usefulness.

Lawrence Welk

Saturday October 17

We took advantage of the fine weather to enjoy a seniors' bus tour of fall foliage. Ben, Marie, Sarah, Richard and I boarded the bus early this morning and we returned tired but happy at dinner time this evening.

Our tour took us from Burlington up past the escarpment and then on the backroads to the town of Alton. Although the trees along our route are just a little past their prime, their colours were still magnificent in the bright sunshine.

In Alton, a tributary of the Credit River, known locally as Shaw's Creek, flows through the centre of town. This fast-flowing stream once provided power to the many mills that lined it, including Dod's Mill, now the Millcroft Inn.

We enjoyed a delicious lunch in the dining room of the inn. The dining room and the rooms at the back of the inn look over a beautiful waterfall that plunges 7 metres to the stream below.

As we ate we were enthralled by two hot-air balloons that passed overhead allowing the passengers a spectacular view.

The ride home through Cheltenham, Terra Cotta and Norval was a delightful end to a most enjoyable day.

Sunday October 18

The Lord is in his holy temple: let all the earth keep silence before him.

Habakkuk 2:20

Monday October 19

The month of October is a sports fan's idea of heaven. The baseball World Series is underway, the football season is in full swing, and the hockey season has begun.

Almost any day or night through these few weeks you can catch a game on the television, and often two or three games simultaneously.

Bruce has complained for a few days that he has had a sore hand. Marg rather unsympathetically remarked that it was probably from overuse of the TV remote control.

Some days it's hard to get any sympathy at all.

Tuesday October 20

We see things not as they are, but as we are.

Wednesday October 21

Nothing lowers the level of conversation more than raising the voice.

Thursday October 22

Life and death are parts of the same great adventure. Do not fear to die and do not shrink from the joy of life.

Friday October 23

My son-in-law John passed along this amusing story.

While out visiting his parishioners one afternoon, the minister knocked on the door of a church member but got no response.

He could hear footsteps so he was a little annoyed. Leaving his calling card he wrote "Revelation 3:20: 'Behold, I stand at the door, and knock: if any man hear my voice, and open the door, I will come in.'"

Following the Sunday service the lady on whose door the minister had knocked gave him her card, which read "Genesis 3:10: 'I heard thy voice in the garden, and I was afraid, because I was naked; and I hid myself.'"

Saturday October 24

The strong winds of last evening almost cleared the trees of their remaining leaves. When I looked out the window this morning it brought the reality of the winter that is coming all too quickly.

These lines from William Knowles come to mind.

In time November's surly blast
Will lay our forest bare,
And bleak December will ensue
To scatter what was there.

But spring again will usher in
A new enchanting morn,
And once again the leaves will come
Our forest to adorn.

Sunday October 25

In Him we live, and move, and have our being.

Acts 17:28

Monday October 26

What matters is not the number of hours you put in, but how much you put in the hours.

Tuesday October 27

Several years ago in the town of Milton, 5-year-old Deidre Scholtz was diagnosed with aplastic anemia. Her only hope was a bone-marrow transplant, but none of her family members were a match for this very sick little girl.

In an emotional plea, the parents asked that people from the town be tested as possible donors. They expected 200 to 300 people at the clinics. Twenty-five hundred friends and neighbours turned out to be tested and members of the community raised $99,700 in 30 days to pay for the testing procedures.

A compatible donor was found and Deidre received the life-saving transfusion.

As her mother said, "It's hard to thank 35,000 people."

Wednesday October 28

In prosperity our friends know us; in adversity we know our friends.

Thursday October 29

Success is getting what you want; happiness is wanting what you get.

Friday October 30

Bruce and his two youngest grandchildren spent this evening getting ready for Halloween. Bethany is very excited about this special day and she was fairly dancing as her grandpa set about to carve the pumpkin. Michael, her young brother, was probably unaware of the significance of pumpkin carving, but he was more than anxious to be involved, his little fingers coming precariously close to the carving knife on several occasions.

Bruce found a very clever way to keep him occupied. After scooping the "guts" out of the pumpkin, he put them into a bowl and gave them to Michael. Although the seeds and the stringy pulp soon attached themselves to every part of this little boy, he enjoyed every second of it and it allowed his grandpa to carve a spectacular Jack-o-Lantern.

Halloween is for kids (and Bruce).

Saturday October 31

To taffy pulls and pleasures gay…
Quaint joys that vanished yesterday.
Oh, just to span the years between
And go back home for Halloween!

November

Sunday November 1

Almighty God, our heavenly Father, we re-member before thee all thy servants who have served thee faithfully in their generations and have entered into rest, beseeching thee to give us grace so to follow in their steps, that with them we may be partakers of thy heavenly kingdom; through Jesus Christ our Lord. Amen.

Collect for All Saints' Day
The Book of Common Prayer

Monday November 2

Eugene Klein, at one time the owner of the San Diego Chargers Football team and a race horse, "Tanks Prospect," was asked the difference between owning a race horse and a football team.

"The biggest difference," Klein answered, "is that after a horse wins a big race he won't come into my office the next day and ask to renegoti-ate his contract."

Tuesday November 3

I am inspired by the accomplishments of elderly friends. As I struggle with my computer class I find this story one to hold on to.

Daisy Sands Rittgers was a freshman at Eastern Illinois University in 1927. She was doing extremely well in her courses when illness and then the stock market crash forced her to withdraw from school.

Teachers in those days did not need to have a university degree, and so Daisy looked for, and found, a job teaching in a school in Illinois.

Time passed, and Daisy married and raised a family while continuing her teaching career.

Finally, at age 75 she retired. All through her career, though, and after her retirement, she felt that something had been left unfinished. And so it was that in the summer of 1996 Daisy enrolled once more at Eastern Illinois University, working hard to complete the courses that would grant her a university degree.

It was with great pride on Sunday August 4, 1996, that Daisy Sands Rittgers proudly walked across the stage to a standing ovation from her classmates, family, friends and staff where the "Board of Governors' Degree" was conferred— some 69 years after she had started.

Wednesday November 4

Courage is leaving a restaurant where you have just dined without leaving a tip. Temerity is going back there for lunch the next day.

Thursday November 5

I enjoyed this small excerpt from *The American Woman's Home* by Catherine E. Beecher and Harriet Beecher Stowe, published in 1869.

These words are as wise and true today as they were then.

As society gradually shakes off the remnants of barbarism…a truer estimate is formed of women's duties, and of the measure of intellect requisite for the proper discharge of them. Let any man of sense and discernment become the member of a large household, in which a well-educated and pious woman is endeavoring systematically to discharge her multiform duties; let him fully comprehend her cares, difficulties and perplexities; and it is probable he would coincide in the opinion that no statesman, at the head of a nations affairs, had more frequent calls for wisdom, firmness, tact, discrimination, prudence and versatility of talent, than such a woman.

Friday November 6

Marshall is a great sports fan and he is interested in little-known sports facts. For those of you who may be playing Trivial Pursuit, these unusual details may come in handy.

Playing golf was once banned in Scotland, its country of origin. The ban was issued in 1457 because the government felt "the game uses up the leisure time of the people."

The most one-sided game in football history was played October 17, 1916. Georgia Tech humiliated Cumberland College 220–0.

Actor William Bendix, once a batboy for the New York Yankees, was fired for smuggling hot dogs and pop into the clubhouse for Babe Ruth, who was battling a weight problem at the time. Years later Bendix starred as the famous ballplayer in *The Babe Ruth Story*.

Dave Winfield was charged with cruelty to animals after a ball that he hit killed a seagull that was flying overhead during a game being played in Toronto. (The charges were later dropped.)

Saturday November 7

The Greeks said grandly in their tragic phrase, "Let no one be called happy till his death"; to which I would say "Let no one, till his death, be called unhappy."

Elizabeth Barrett Browning

Sunday November 8

The Lord seeth not as man seeth; for man looketh on the outward appearance, but the Lord looketh on the heart.

1 Samuel 16:7

Monday November 9

People who write the most interesting and effective letters never answer letters; they answer people.

Tuesday November 10

If you put forth your best you need not fear the worst.

Wednesday November 11

REMEMBRANCE DAY

When World War I ended at the eleventh hour of the eleventh day of the eleventh month, many believed that the world would never again see such a terrible loss of life. History proved them wrong, and the losses suffered in World War II were devastating almost beyond endurance.

It is my prayer today that somehow, some way, no family shall ever have to bear the loss of a loved one in conflict and that our world shall see "peace in our time."

Thursday November 12

My grandsons Mickey and Geoffrey are very fond of cats. They offered these words of Helen Power to explain:

There are a lot of good reasons why a cat makes an ideal pet. Cats are quiet. They need very little space, a minimum of care and they are clean. A cat won't attack the mailman or eat the drapes—although he may climb the drapes to see how the room looks from the ceiling.

(From: The Biggest Little Cat Book in the World—Grossett and Dunlop)

Friday November 13

This interesting note appeared on the church bulletin board during the minister's illness.

God is good.
Dr. Lockhart is better.

Saturday November 14

Relativity is why the red light is twice as long as the green light even though both are 20 seconds.

Sunday November 15

My Father, for another night
Of quiet sleep and rest,
For all the joy of morning light,
Thy holy name be blest.

Now with the new-born day I give
Myself anew to Thee,
That as Thou willest I may live,
And what Thou willest be.

Rev. Sir H.W. Baker

Monday November 16

As I sat in our church yesterday I was admiring the beautiful stained glass windows and their incredible colours as the light shone through them.

Did you know that stained glass was brought to Canada in the mid-1800s by immigrants wishing to maintain a nostalgic link with Europe? By the 1890s companies all across Canada were making stained glass windows of all types, many using their own designs.

Hand-blown stained glass from Britain, France and Germany is still the best. Sand, soda, lime and a few added minerals are transformed into the glass in a tremendous range of colours; one factory in France produces 4,000 different hues, tints and tones.

A stained glass window begins with a sketch on paper that the artist wishes to create. The glass is chosen and then cut to size. The window is constructed inside a lead border by fitting the glass, piece by piece, into lengths of grooved lead, each cut to fit exactly. The joints are then soldered front and back, and the work is cemented, thus making it waterproof.

It is one of the world's most creative art forms and many of the most beautiful works are found in churches. They are there for all to enjoy.

Tuesday November 17

You must change with the times unless you are big enough to change the times.

Wednesday November 18

We are never so generous as when giving advice.

Duc de La Rochefoucauld

Thursday November 19

This is Thanksgiving Day for my many American friends. In honour of this happy family celebration I offer these "Reasons for Thanksgiving" from Edith Shaw Butter.

To have food enough and a place to dwell
To have work to do and to do it well…
To find the comfort when things go wrong
In a bit of prayer or snatch of song…
To know the pleasure a kind act brings
To see the beauty in simple things…
To know good books and share their worth,
To plant bright flowers in rich brown earth…
To have true friends…this is living
And reason enough for Thanksgiving.

Friday November 20

Our family has a proud Irish ancestry. Over the years we heard many a blessing from my father, and I offer you just a few to enjoy today.

May the road rise up to meet you, may the wind be always at your back, may the sun shine warm upon your face, may the rain fall softly on your fields, and until we meet again may God hold you in the palm of His hand.

May you have warm words on a cold evening,
a full moon on a dark night,
and a smooth road all the way to your door.

May your right hand always be stretched out in friendship, but never in want.

May your soul be in heaven an hour before the devil knows you're dead.

May leprechauns strew happiness wherever you walk each day, and Irish angels smile on you all along the way.

When you die, may you be buried in a coffin made from the wood of a 100-year-old oak, which I will plant tomorrow.

Saturday November 21

I will be spending today working on my computer, trying to make sense of the text and the class notes that I have made. Thankfully, I won't be alone. Several of my classmates have taken it upon themselves to come over to my home and give me some extra help.

I believe that I have become a class "project." These wonderful young people seem to think that it is their duty to make sure that I pass this course. Whenever we are doing practical work in class nearly every student will come by my terminal to be sure that I have understood the instructions and that I am able to carry out the given tasks. They have even been so kind as to include me in their after-class coffee times at the nearby doughnut shop.

Perhaps they consider me to be a surrogate grandparent, but whatever their reasons I will be forever grateful and indebted to these kind young people.

Sunday November 22

So teach us to number our days, that we may apply our hearts into wisdom.

Psalms 90:12

Monday November 23

Last evening brought our first snowfall. We awoke this morning to a white lawn and a radio report of treacherous road conditions.

We Canadians are a funny lot. We spend four to five months of every year driving in snow, sleet, freezing rain—days and days of dreadful driving situations. People drive, for the most part, using great care and caution. Then we enjoy summer and it's as if everything ever known about driving in poor weather has left us. Comes the first snow and people are all over the road, driving too quickly, smacking into one another and causing general rush-hour mayhem. We can only hope that the chaos of today will be a reminder to slow down tomorrow. Ah, the joys of a snowy Canadian winter!

Tuesday November 24

Wisdom is ofttimes nearer when we stoop than when we soar.

William Wordsworth

Wednesday November 25

A study has shown what many of us already felt was true: children from broken homes are themselves more likely to get divorced.

Not surprisingly, children of divorced parents have a lower commitment to marriage. They tend to be hesitant and cautious about marriage during adolescence, often saying that they won't marry. They often do marry, though, and they marry at an earlier age. Because they fear failure in their marriage they withhold a full commitment.

According to the study, a female whose parents have been divorced stands the greatest chance of divorcing in her marriage. As a rule, when she marries, a woman's lifestyle changes more than her husband's.

The couple usually live near his job, socialize more often with his friends and, if they have children, she bears the brunt of caring for them. The woman has to make the greater adjustment, and she is not likely to make that adjustment if she's not fully committed to the marriage.

I guess that my generation is old-fashioned enough to hope that "marriage for life" will become popular once again and that children will be raised in a home where love is a lifetime commitment.

Thursday November 26

Bruce made an interesting observation at dinner this evening.

"Ask any man 'Where did you buy these pork-chops?' and he will answer 'At the supermarket.' Ask a woman the same question and she will reply 'Why, what's the matter with them?'"

I do believe he's right.

Friday November 27

Some men have thousands of reasons why they cannot do what they want to, when all they need is one reason why they can.

Dr. Willis R. Whitney

Saturday November 28

In these days when chivalry, although not dead, seems mortally wounded it is sometimes necessary to use ingenuity.

My friend Mavis has an elderly friend who has little trouble getting a seat on a bus. She hands her cane to the person closest to her that she deems capable of standing and says "Would you mind holding this so that I can hang on with two hands?"

Sunday November 29

This is the first Sunday in Advent and I would like to share with you the collect for this day.

Almighty God, give us grace that we may cast away the works of darkness and put upon us the armour of light, now in the time of this mortal life, in which thy Son Jesus Christ came to visit us in great humility; that in the last day, when he shall come again in his glorious Majesty to judge both the quick and the dead, we may rise to the life immortal; through him that liveth and reigneth with thee and the Holy Spirit, now and ever. Amen.

Monday November 30

One of my daughters' greatest pleasures, as children, was opening each day of the Advent Calendar as it led to Christmas Day. Often the calendars contained small pieces of chocolate, which added to their enjoyment.

Although the calendars are becoming more difficult to find, I located enough to give to each great-grandchild. I hope they will add to the children's enjoyment of the coming of Christmas.

December

Tuesday December 1

Home is where affections bind
Gentle hearts in unison;
Where the voices are all kind
Holding sweet communion.

Home is where the heart can rest
Safe from darkening sorrow;
Where the friends we love the best
Brighten every morrow!

Home is where the friends that love
To our hearts are given;
Where the blessings from above
Make it seem a heaven!

Home is where the stars will shine
In the skies above us;
Peeping brightly through the vine,
Trained by those who love us!

Yes 'tis home, where smiles of cheer
Wreathe the brows that greet us;
And the one of all most dear
Ever comes to meet us!

Wednesday December 2

This is a very busy month of the year. Along with Christmas baking, shopping for gifts and tree decorating, this time is often one of the most hectic socially. Companies large and small often hold gatherings for employees and their families and, as well, many people host their own neighbourhood gatherings to celebrate the joys of the season.

How easy it is to forget or ignore those friends and relatives who are shut-ins. A visit with them, no matter how brief, can bring pleasure to those who are unable to be out and around.

No one wants to feel forgotten. Please take time to visit.

Thursday December 3

Going to church doesn't make you a Christian any more than going to the garage makes you an automobile.

Friday December 4

The sending and receiving of Christmas cards remains one of my favourite traditions of the season. Although not as popular as it once was, perhaps due to the rising cost of postage, a Christmas card is a chance to renew old friendships and perhaps begin new ones.

I look forward each day to the postman's arrival to hear from my many friends the news that they send from across Canada and around the world.

In my own cards as well, I try to include a personal note to each person. For some, this may be our only communication of the year, and yet for each of us it is an important tie.

Some people choose to write a many-page "generic" letter to include in their cards. While these letters are always interesting, I find them just a little too impersonal for me. As well, I have more time than many and I truly enjoy writing. Each card gives me a chance to enjoy memories shared with the receiver.

Marg and I spent several hours at the mall choosing our cards, and now comes the joyful task of writing them. I hope this is a happy job for you as well.

Saturday December 5

Tonight is St. Nicholas Eve, a time of expectation for children in many countries in Europe. December 6 is the feast day of St. Nicholas, who lived in the fourth century. As archbishop of the metropolitan church of Myra, Lycia, he became known for his good works and sumptuous gifts.

In fact his gift-giving was so renowned that it became the custom, when celebrating the feast of St. Nicholas, to follow his example by giving gifts as well.

Probably because of the closeness of the two dates, the feast of St. Nicholas became associated with the feast of Christmas. This is how the custom of exchanging gifts at Christmas came to be associated with the good works of St. Nicholas. However, many Europeans still reserve St. Nicholas Eve as the day for lavish gift giving, most particularly to the children.

Sunday December 6

So teach us to number our days, that we may apply our hearts unto wisdom.

Psalms 90:12

Monday December 7

As a final incentive before giving up a difficult task, try to imagine it successfully accomplished by someone you violently dislike.

Tuesday December 8

Marg and I went shopping in downtown Toronto today. Each time I visit the city I am amazed by the size of the buildings and the number of people that are hurrying along the sidewalks to goodness knows where.

Charles Dickens visited Toronto in 1842 and wrote:

The country round this town being very flat, is bare of scenic interest; but the town itself is full of life and motion, bustle, business and improvement. The streets are well paved, and lighted with gas; the houses are large and good; the shops excellent. Many of them have a display of goods in their windows such as may be seen in thriving towns in England; and there are some which would do no discredit to the metropolis itself.

Wednesday December 9

One year my daughter Julia decided to knit socks as Christmas gifts. She started with the best of intentions, but it actually took her nearly another whole year to complete the pair that she made for her father.

When she called her dad to see how they were, we all laughed at his reply:

"Why, Julia, they are really magnificent, but just the least bit tight under the arms."

Thursday December 10

My grandson Marshall remarked today that the secret of a clean desk is a mammoth wastebasket.

Friday December 11

A man without imagination is like a bird without wings.

Saturday December 12

Many of us on a fixed budget find gift giving at Christmas a considerable strain on the pocketbook. Finding just the right present for a minimal cost can be challenging. My friend and neighbour Lila MacGuiness and I spent today making gifts that we hope our families will enjoy.

Over the year we collected hundreds of small pine cones that we let dry. These we have glued on styrofoam rings and sprinkled with green and red sparkles. We've added a bow of 1 1/2" red and green plaid ribbon and a large red candle, and there we have a lovely decoration for a fireplace mantel or even a bathroom countertop.

We had a wonderful time making them and I'm sure our families will enjoy our ingenuity.

Sunday December 13

And behold, thou shalt conceive in thy womb, and bring forth a son and shalt call his name Jesus.

Luke 1:31

Monday December 14

It would not seem like Christmas,
Without the Christmas lights…
They glow so softly radiant,
And glorify the night.

Tuesday December 15

We do not have to choose our favourite among the seasons. It is only necessary to rejoice in the beauty of their differences.

Evelyn Lauder

Wednesday December 16

You do not grow old; you become old by not growing.

Thursday December 17

Ninety-five years ago today Orville Wright made man's first airplane flight. It was the culmination of a dream shared by men for centuries.

Leonardo da Vinci said, "For once you have tasted flight, you will walk the earth with your eyes turned skyward, for there you have been and there you long to return."

Friday December 18

Maturity is the art of living in peace with that which we cannot change.

Saturday December 19

The Christmas Bazaar was held at our church today and it was a huge success. Each year the parishioners donate generously of their time—and home-made crafts—so that we will make enough money to provide a happy Christmas for the less fortunate families in the area.

A few years ago a very dear friend of mine made a magnificent pine cone Christmas tree adorned with tiny white bulbs, red bows and white beads, to be used as a raffle prize. Betty died before Christmas that year but her friends made sure that her gift would be remembered by raising more than $1,500 in the raffle.

This year the winner brought back the tree, suggesting that we raffle it again and continue to do so each year, if the winner agrees.

I can't think of a better way to remember this selfless lady.

Sunday December 20

How I enjoy the Christmas hymns. Here is one of my favourites.

Once in Royal David's City
Stood a lowly cattle shed.
Where a mother laid her baby
In a manger for his bed;
Mary was that mother mild,
Jesus Christ her little child.

Monday December 21

The young people of our area completed their Christmas collecting of tinned goods this evening. Each year the local high school organizes a food drive to make sure that no families will be short of food for the holiday season.

This year's group added something special. The collectors dressed in costumes from the early part of the century and sang carols as they moved from home to home.

When people are critical of today's youth they obviously haven't met these fine young people.

Tuesday December 22

If you look for beauty you will find it. If you listen for the voice of truth, you will hear it. If you love, you will be loved.

Wednesday December 23

The most valuable gift you can give another is a good example.

Thursday December 24

For God so loved the world, that he gave his only begotten Son, that whosoever believeth in him should not perish, but have everlasting life.

John 3:16

Friday December 25

How I enjoy the Christmas story as we hear it each year on this special morning. As our pastor read the words I had only to close my eyes and I could hear my husband George as he would say, "And this will be a sign for you; you will find a baby wrapped in cloths, and lying in a manger."

A very Merry Christmas to you all.

Saturday December 26

How I do love Christmas dinner. Last evening our family enjoyed its usual delicious, noisy affair as family members gathered from near and far to celebrate our Saviour's birth.

What I enjoy most is watching the children. Their unrepressed excitement and enthusiasm makes a very old lady feel young again, even if it's only for today!

Sunday December 27

For unto us a child is born, unto us a son is given.

Isaiah 9:6

Monday December 28

Ideals are like stars; you will not succeed in touching them with your hands. But like the seafaring man on the desert of waters, you choose them as your guides, and following them you will reach your destiny.

Tuesday December 29

My sister Sarah had a good laugh today. Opening her mailbox, she found two notes awaiting her. The first was from a neighbour: "There was no one home when I rang so I left your Christmas gift in the mailbox." The second note read, "Thank you for the tin of shortbread cookies. They were delicious." It was signed by the mailman.

Wednesday December 30

This is the time of year to reflect on the days past. "Did I accomplish my goals? What objectives can I set for myself in the coming year?"

I hope that you too can look back on the year with a feeling of pride in your accomplishments and of hope for happiness in the year to come.

Thursday December 31

I wish to each and every one a very Happy New Year.